WHAT READERS ARE SAYING...

"David Roy Newby's techniques will enable you to build a strong legacy for your family... and find and fix the cracks that likely exist in your current legacy/estate plan."

**-David Green,
Founder and CEO, Hobby Lobby**

"Men, especially as heads of family, as business owners, are alone on a lonely journey of identity and creators of extreme wealth. Every single owner, head of family office, estate planner, and advisor to the wealthy needs to read 'Beyond Billions'!"

**-Robin Coady Smith,
Succession Planner to
Billionaires, PrCio.com**

"David Roy Newby's 'Beyond Billions' is beyond inspirational. It's transformative, and in all the right ways. Having come from a fatherless home myself, his personal stories resonate well with me. He touches on ancient, fundamental elements of wealth creation and preservation that are ignored by the vast majority of estate planners today. Don't

delay. Read 'Beyond Billions' and take action today. No matter your endeavors, I promise you: it will greatly benefit you, & everyone who knows you."

-Alexander Doak,
Philippines entrepreneur

"'Beyond Billions' is a provocative, paradigm-challenging look at the all too common frustration and failure by hard-charging, high-achieving entrepreneurs and top executives with regard to family influence, transferring wisdom, not just wealth. In a complete consideration of what you are doing and why you are doing it, this has a place. Making, taking, and accumulating is all fine. I am Ayn Rand-ian about enlightened self-interest and earned privilege. But there is also something, as David puts it, beyond millions or billions, beyond scorekeeping. Tapping King Solomon as inspiration, he has done an interesting job of raising both philosophical and practical questions."

**Dan Kennedy,
consultant to multi-billion dollar companies
& author; www.DanKennedy.com**

"The principles discussed in this book give us a solid strategy for creating a lasting legacy *that will impact lives for generations to come. Being a father to 7 children, we started a family foundation in 2008 with the goal of teaching our kids while simultaneously giving them opportunities to apply what they've learned. I'm always looking for resources that will aid us in communicating with and teaching our children so we can continue building our family legacy. 'Beyond Billions' is a great resource!"*

-Kevin Thompson, co-founder, Relationship Accelerator Network

"This book is a MUST READ for anyone looking to secure their family's financial (and even spiritual) legacy. In 'Beyond Billions,' David Roy Newby lays out a clear, easy to follow plan for creating a lasting legacy of multigenerational wealth and shared values within your family. David's unique concept of holding annual "Family Vault Meetings" is something I've never heard anyone else talk about, and I personally plan on doing one with my own children soon. Most wealthy people only look at estate planning from a tax & financial perspective. However, armed with this groundbreaking book, you

will be able to secure and ensure your family's TRUE legacy for generations to come."

**-Eric Graham,
Marketing consultant to multiple $100M+ companies & founder of <u>ConversionDoctor.com</u>**

"I am so grateful that David took the time to figure this all out. You can tell that David has done his homework on this important topic and the research he shares astounds me! I want to do better with my legacy and this book will be a great resource. I've seen families crumble because of a poorly planned transitions or spoil the next generation with too much money and too little responsibility. This book lays out a clear and easy to follow system to make sure your legacy thrives long after you've moved on. Thank you for this gift David, the legacy you are creating is massive!"

-David Boufford, creator of Good News Network

"I've spent countless hours over the years in the personal space of some of the wealthiest families in America. I learned simply by observing them that children of successful parents can suffer *self-destruction fueled by various dysfunctions born of a rich upbringing devoid of appreciation for what the last generation accomplished for the next's benefit. It takes work, foresight, communication, and planning in order to avoid the pitfalls mentioned above. 'Beyond Billions' highlights how those areas can be addressed and navigated in order to nurture the most desirable outcomes of generational wealth and happiness."*

**-Joey Atlas,
creator of SculptAFit Home Gym**

"As a marketing consultant having turned huge companies around, I'm impressed. David Roy Newby teaches you principles that enable you to not only have money, but grow the money you have and to transfer the skillsets to your children. Is that important? It's one of the most vital things you can do. This book is essential not only to read but to implement."

**-Joel Bauer, best-selling author
and master perceptionist,
www.PersuasionFoundation.com**

TREASURE ISLANDS

Your Guide to Protecting Your Wealth with Gold, Silver, and Digital Sound Money... in the Philippines and Beyond

David Roy Newby

Dearborn, MI

Published by StraightArrow Press LLC
3319 Greenfield Rd. #369, Dearborn MI 48120, USA

Treasure Islands: Your Guide to Protecting Your Wealth with Gold, Silver, and Digital Sound Money… in the Philippines and Beyond

Legal Disclaimer: the information in this book is not presented as a source of tax, financial, or legal advice. You should not rely on statements or representations made within the book or by any externally referenced sources. If you need tax, legal, or financial advice upon which you intend to rely in the course of your business or legal affairs, consult a competent, independent professional.

The contents of this book should not be taken as financial or investment advice, or as an offer to buy or sell any securities, fund, type of fund, or financial instruments. It should not be taken as an endorsement or recommendation of any particular company or individual, and no responsibilities can be taken for any inaccuracies, omissions, or errors.

The author and publisher do not assume any responsibility for actions or nonactions taken by people who have read this book, and no one shall be entitled to a claim for detrimental reliance based upon any information provided or expressed herein. Your use of any information provided here does not constitute any type of contractual relationship between yourself and the provider(s) of this information. The author and publisher hereby disclaim all responsibility and liability for all use of any information provided in this book.

2nd Edition ©2023 by Noor Yeshua Trust
All rights reserved.

Reproduction or translation of any part of this work beyond that permitted by Section 107 or 108 of the 1976 United States Copyright Act without permission of the copyright owner is unlawful. Requests for permission or further information should be addressed to Noor Yeshua Trust.
ISBN: 979-8-3507-1971-0

Paperback Edition
124 pages

DEDICATION

I dedicate this book to Filipinos who
are committed to rising above all
obstacles to achieve their dreams.

And to my mother Violet, who brought me to
the Philippines in 1984 as a 10 year old boy.

Lastly, to God for birthing in my heart
a love for Filipinos and a desire to serve
them in achieving their financial plans.

Maraming salamat!
(*"Thank You"* in Filipino)

CONTENTS

INTRODUCTION 1

CHAPTER 1 9
Why Conventional Wisdom Stinks

CHAPTER 2 27
"Something's Wrong With the World Today…"

CHAPTER 3 43
All That Glitters Isn't Gold

CHAPTER 4 61
Protect Yourself from the WEF Agenda 2030 & Other Threats

CHAPTER 5 89
"Get Back IN There and Sell, Sell, SELL!!!"

CHAPTER 6 105
Conclusion: So What is the Golden Opportunity Before You Now?
That depends on you.

RESOURCES 111

INTRODUCTION

Hello! My name is David Newby. If you're reading this in the Philippines, you may be wondering why an American wrote a book for people in the Philippines. Good question.

Before I get to that, let me answer another pressing question: if you live outside the Philippines, you may be wondering, *"Will I benefit from this book, as I don't live in the Philippines?"* Never fear, my friend. You will benefit from every strategy I outline in this book... provided you take action on the information (EXCEPT for Chapter 5 which is specific to Philippines laws about selling gold; simply skip over that, and benefit from the rest of the book).

So, back to why I wrote this book. As a child I grew up in a very abusive household, and when I was 7 my dad tried to kill my mom and caused her to miscarry my second brother, Joseph. She divorced him, and we moved every 3 months so my dad couldn't find us.

During this time my mom, brother, and I survived on $503 a month, which is equal to about PHP 2,000 in today's money.

I was quite angry at the world during this time in my life; I was angry at my dad because he caused our family to fall apart, angry that he and my mom couldn't work things out, and angry that we were poor all of the sudden.

In the midst of this chaos, when I was 10 my mother brought me and my brother to live in the Philippines as medical missionaries in the summer of 1984. That summer in Bagong Barrio, Caloocan changed my life forever.

In the U.S. I was complaining that my socks had holes in them and I had to wear $2 plastic shoes from the drugstore; I met friends with no shoes at all. I complained about doing chores, and I met a friend who had to work at 4AM every morning before school to help his family pay the bills. I complained about my dad being gone, and then I met kids my own age whose parents had sold them for food because their families were literally starving to death.

What a wake-up call! God taught me to be thankful for what I have through my Filipino friends' contentment and gladness in the midst of deep poverty.

But I learned something else too: extreme generosity. It blew my mind that someone making PHP 30/month (a little over $1/day) would spend PHP 5 to buy us a marienda just because we were their guests. That's over 15% of their income!

Needless to say, I returned home from the Philippines a changed person. In fact, I told my mom when we got home that I'd marry a Filipina one day. I forgot that I said it, and guess what? I met my Filipina wife 11 years later at a nursing home in Detroit (we were both working there, not patients - thank the Lord Jesus) and fulfilled my prophecy by marrying her. I'm grateful to report that our 21 year marriage produced two sons that are an immense blessing to my life.

So, how did this book come about again?

Two key incidents led to this book being in your hands: first, 13 months after marrying my beautiful Filipina wife I got laid off from my job suddenly. That helped me realize at a young age that job security only exists in your mind, so I committed to make myself *"layoff-proof for life"* to provide a better life for me and my family.

By God's grace, in the first 11 years of being in business, I was able to semi-retire at the age of 32 and write my first book, "*Why Didn't Anyone Teach Me This?*" Since then, I've published two other books, spoken to 122 billionaires, and shared the stage with David Green of Hobby Lobby and one of the Rockefeller's. Not too shabby for a poor welfare kid from the hills of Chattanooga, Tennessee!

The second incident that led to this book being in your hands is a trade mission I went on to the Philippines in 2006. While there, I got a vision to help Filipinos both spiritually and economically. I wrote out a game plan to become an inverse tither (to give 80% of my income to charities to build God's Kingdom), with the majority of the funds being invested into microfinance and infrastructure to empower "*the least of these*" among us.

The reason I'm publishing this second edition of this book in 2023 is that the World Economic Forum plans to steal all your wealth by the year 2030 (they call this plan "*Agenda 2030*" or "*The Great Reset*" and its' catchphrase is 'You'll own nothing, and you'll be happy'). If you value your economic freedom at ALL, I'm sure you want to preserve your wealth, and chapter 4 of this book gives you 4 key economic strategies to do so.

God has provided ALL the resources we need to prosper right in our own backyards, so I plan to help as many people in the Philippines as possible learn how to create wealth in precious metals with this book. Are you ready to *"go for the gold"* in your own life? Great- let's get started!!

Who This Book Is For

This book is for you if you fit one of the following descriptions:

1. You're a wise investor or business owner considering buying precious metals to either grow or protect your wealth, in the midst of both current and future potential economic dangers.

2. You're a miner or pawnshop owner looking to maximize your profit when both buying and selling gold and silver.

3. You're a current holder of some precious metals, and want to know how and when to sell some of it as safely and profitably as possible.

4. You're concerned about growing inflation, banks failing, the WEF's Agenda 2030, and global uncertainty, and you want to know how MUCH crypto and precious metals you should buy, and HOW to buy and hold those assets to best preserve your wealth.

With this book, I'll make you aware of the global financial trends that affect you today and threaten your economic safety in the future if you don't take action. This book will also empower you to adopt the right mindset to deal with these dangers in full confidence that you're doing everything in your power to protect yourself and your family's financial health.

To be successful in any endeavor, you must begin with accurate thinking. After reading this book, you'll know the rules of the global financial game and be equipped to win big.

We'll cover both historic and recent financial trends that affect your pocketbook, and you'll also discover the BEST ways to invest in gold and silver in the Philippines.

I figure you bought this book because you want to do better than average, and I commit to help you with that. Most importantly, I'm going to show you ways to protect the money you already have and all the money you'll ever amass in the future. Sound good to you?

If yes, then you're reading the right book. I don't claim to have all the answers, but I do have a blueprint for success that anyone can follow. Again, you WILL create greater wealth using the strategies in this book- that is, if you don't let your fears get the best of you.

After reading this book you will have the basic tools necessary to protect your wealth and have the opportunity to grow your wealth massively with gold and silver.

You'll discover...

- The historic and recent trends that show why owning gold and silver is the ultimate protection for your wealth, and how to use this book to NOW benefit from the largest wealth transfer in the history of the world

- Why following conventional wisdom is making you poor, and the mindset you must adopt to improve your family's lifestyle

- The good, bad, and the ugly truth about consumer debt

- How to invest in precious metals profitably, easily, and safely

- The simple steps to build wealth faster than a speeding bullet

- How to protect your wealth now and for your family's future generations.

- When to know it's time to sell your precious metals for maximum profit

- The 3 key strategies you must employ to safely sell Philippines treasure gold (covered in Chapter 5: this only applies to Philippines readers)

Before we get into how bleak the global financial picture is, first I want to empower you to deal with the information with some sound, accurate thinking. Without the right mindset, receiving bad news can discourage you and even put you in such a state of fear that you're afraid to do anything to protect yourself. Neither of us want that for you.

I'm sure you're ready to implement your own solution to ensure the prosperity of your life for you and your family, so let's get started now - helping you optimize your thinking.

CHAPTER 1

Why Conventional Wisdom Stinks

In my first book *"Why Didn't Anyone Teach Me This?"*, I used the Problem-Agitate-Solve marketing model to lay out all the financial challenges people face with some scary, sobering statistics before offering them great solutions to each of those challenges.

A couple years after my book came out, I learned some information that was so shocking and disheartening to me that I didn't take action to address the challenge for over 2 months. Also since that time, I've learned a lot about fear in the spiritual realm.

Based on these 2 things, I'm going to empower you with some accurate thinking and hope before laying out the financial challenges you face and the best ways to address them with precious metals in the coming chapters. That way you'll be BEST prepared to deal with any bad news you receive in the future- from me or anyone else!

Also in my first book, I outlined the financial statistic that 9 out of 10 people in the world retire broke. If you think if only you can move to a richer country you'll have a greater chance of financial success, you're wrong. Even in America, the richest country in the world today, 90% of people retire broke.

I'm sure you agree with me that most people don't want to end up with that financial future. For you to avoid being one of the 9 who retire broke, it's important to look into what most people do during their lives to end up with those horrible results. Then I'll show you how to avoid that fate for yourself.

So, where's the best place to find hope and get accurate information in order to have positive, accurate thinking? The Bible.

Don't be deceived into thinking the Bible only deals with *"spiritual stuff"* and has nothing to offer you regarding creating wealth with precious metals. The Bible actually says more about money than any other topic! Here are just a few examples:

Jesus, who many people of all religions consider to be one of the most enlightened people ever to live on Earth, said *"Don't store up for yourselves treasures on earth, where moth and rust destroy, and where thieves break in and steal."*

King Solomon, the richest man who ever lived- he amassed over $2 TRILLION dollars of gold at today's value of $2,000/oz in his lifetime- said *"the blessing of the Lord brings wealth, and He adds no trouble to it."*

King Solomon also said *"the fear of the Lord is the beginning of wisdom"* and *"commit to the Lord whatever you do, and your plans will succeed."* If you want to do well financially and have a hope for your future, doesn't it make sense to listen to what the richest man who ever lived has to say about it? Of course!

*To put King Solomon's wealth in perspective, his wealth in his gold holdings alone was equal to the combined net worth of HALF of the world's billionaires today including Michael Jordan, Henry Sy, and Elon Musk. So, read Ecclesiastes and Proverbs every day before you read books written about billionaires to get the best wisdom & business training.

Now that we've established the Bible is the BEST place to find wealth-building information and good news, the first action you need to take on your road to wealth using this book (or any other book, for that matter) is to change the way you think about money. Why? Consider this simple formula.

Beliefs → Thoughts → Actions → Results.

Our beliefs lead to our thoughts. Our thoughts lead to our actions. And our actions produce our results.

How can we start to think more prosperously? By replacing beliefs we were taught growing up that limit us, with beliefs that are empowering. Solomon became a trillionaire by using wisdom that came from the fear of the Lord, and you can be sure any belief you have that disagrees with God's Word in the Bible is limiting your financial results.

Prosperous people aren't any better than you or smarter than you; they're simply applying more of God's principles in their finances. It's critical you adopt the thoughts and beliefs of the prosperous in order to get their results. If you don't, you'll NEVER improve your life.

There are countless limiting beliefs people accept as truth. Let's deal with the most common ones so you can replace them with accurate, empowering beliefs in your mind. See how many of the limiting beliefs of the poor and middle class you've had in the past that you are now replacing with the truths of God's Word:

The Poor and middle class think:	Prosperous people think:
"I have to work hard to make a lot of money."	"It's easy to create as much wealth as I want."
"Inheriting money or winning the lotto are the two most likely ways to get rich."	"Building businesses and investing the profits wisely is the best way to create wealth."
"The rich are greedy."	"I'm just like everyone else."
"I'd rather have love than money."	"It's not an either or world- it's an AND world."
"It's hard to get rich."	"It's easy to create wealth."
"If someone's getting rich, someone else is losing money and getting poor."	"There is infinite wealth in our world- there's more than enough for everyone."

Did you find you believe some of the thoughts of the poor and middle class? If you did, that's OK. Several years ago I thought many of those thoughts, and I'm glad to tell you I've asked God to renew my mind to think more accurately and He has- and so can you!

Here are some verses in the Bible that guide what prosperous people think about money:

"The blessing of the Lord gives wealth, and He adds no trouble to it." — Proverbs 10:22

"The plans of the diligent lead to profit as surely as haste leads to poverty" — Prov. 21:5

"They that desire to be rich fall into a snare and a trap, but Godliness with contentment is great gain" — 1 Timothy 6:6

"He who pursues righteousness and love finds life, prosperity, and honor" — Proverbs 21:21

"My Father shall give you everything you ask for in My name. I have come that you may have life, and have it more abundantly." — John 16:23, John 10:10

A great litmus test to see if something you believe is true or not is to see if it agrees with the Bible. A great resource to use to see what the Bible says about different topics is http://www.openbible.info/topics/gold — simply type in the topic, see what God's Word has to say about it, and meditate on the accurate verses to renew your mind.

I encourage you to think seriously about your belief system and how it relates to money. Realize that money in and of itself is not good or bad- it's simply a tool. You can use it for good to help yourself and those around you, or you can use it for bad. Someone may have bad intentions of what they want to do with money, but that doesn't make money itself bad. The problem is with their heart.

The second category of limiting beliefs to overcome is conventional wisdom. Would you agree MOST people follow conventional wisdom? I contend that most do.

What is the conventional wisdom about work and money? Go to school and get a good education. Get a safe, secure job and work hard at your career. Invest your retirement funds in the stock market and land. Retire in comfort and enjoy your golden years. That's what people in the Philippines are taught, right?

If conventional wisdom leads people to such bad results, why do most people keep following it? Simple: most of us haven't been taught how to act any better financially.

We can look around and see that most people are broke, and we don't want that. We can see that most people have a lot of debt and are very stressed financially, and we don't want that. It's no wonder most people are broke- we hardly ever meet people who aren't!!!

We're simply modeling the behavior around us, as poor as it is. What else are we to do? First of all, admit to yourself that maybe there's a better way of thinking about things.

I want your target to be prospering, not getting rich. Why? Because we probably all know someone who is rich financially but doesn't have a balanced life. Prosperous is defined in Webster's Dictionary as *"enjoying vigorous and healthy growth: flourishing."* Doesn't it sound wonderful to be flourishing in every area? Make it your target to prosper in every area of your life including your finances. Victory Church has some great

FREE trainings (mp3s and podcasts) on living prosperously at VictoryFort.org.- check it out!

Before you can ever become prosperous, you need to start with an open mind and admit to yourself that what you already know isn't the *"whole truth"* — accept that there is more you need to learn.

There are two great ways to reject conventional wisdom in your own mind to create new beliefs that will lead to new actions and results:

1. Use Walt Disney's rule: look at what 90% of people are doing and do the opposite. Most people aren't successful, so by doing the opposite of them you're applying wisdom. *"I applied my*

heart to what I observed, and I learned from what I saw." — Proverbs 24:32

2. Say affirmations aloud that empower you.

If you're committed to achieving maximum prosperity for you and your family, then say these words with me out loud: *"I NOW prosper in every way- my finances, my health, and my spirituality. I commit to learning whatever I need to learn, and I commit to implement it until I achieve my desired goal."*

Did you just repeat those words out loud with me? If you did, then you just basically agreed with me that conventional wisdom stinks! It's very unconventional to decide to be prosperous- 9 out of 10 people never do.

I want to point out here that you don't have to want to be rich to repeat the above statement. Remember the warnings from 1 Timothy that people that want to be rich fall into snares and traps; your target is to be diligent and wise and for your family to prosper as a result.

Most people will never make the simple decision to prosper. Maybe they were taught that money is bad or that money is the root of all evil (the Bible verse says the LOVE of money is the root of all [kinds of] evil, **not** money itself) or that they don't deserve it.

All of those things are false and limiting beliefs. Maybe you heard such things from your parents or other authority figures while you were growing up. Ask yourself: do those statements agree with God's Word? What were the financial results of the people who said those things? Do you want those results? If their statements don't agree with the Bible or if you don't want their results for yourself, choose to respectfully disagree with those limiting beliefs you were taught.

Before I give you more great empowering beliefs to wrap up this chapter, note that it's NOT disrespectful to your family to reject their beliefs. If your parents taught you to seek God's will and you align your beliefs with God's Word, then choosing to believe God's truth over limiting beliefs honors them!

So, now that we've established that it's vital to replace limiting beliefs with empowering beliefs that agree with God's Word, here are some empowering beliefs that are key for you to adopt in order to maximize your success using the rest of this book and any other resource you invest your time and money in:

First, realize you are rich already. You are God's creation, and He's given you everything you need to prosper already. Filipinos have some of the strongest family ties of any people on the Earth, and consistently Filipinos rank in the top 5% of all countries in happiness. (Interestingly, Americans are in the bottom 15%- it goes to show you that more money doesn't translate to true prosperity.)

Filipinos are rated #1 as the easiest people in the world to get along with, and the Philippines is the 7th most mineral-rich country in the world with the mining sector only being 17% utilized. So there's a lot of untapped gold in them there hills! (that's from "*The Beverly Hillbillies*," a 1950s TV show)

Speaking of gold, Filipinos are some of the most creative people in the world; Napoleon Hill said in "*Think And Grow Rich*" that more gold has been mined from the minds of men than from the ground. So, we can conclude that God gave you a double portion of gold as you're in the Philippines. That's great news!

Second, God loves you and wants you to prosper mightily. "*For I know the plans I have for you*" declares the Lord, "*plans to prosper you and not to harm you, plans to give you hope and a future.*" — Jeremiah 29:11

Third, know that in any crisis there's always the seed of an equivalent or greater benefit. In the next chapter, I'm going to outline a very substantial crisis and I want you to see that as a good thing for you because of the great opportunity it presents to you now.

Fourth, commit to renewing your mind regularly to create new financial results. Do this by reading your Bible (especially Proverbs and Ecclesiastes) regularly and reciting Biblical truths out loud that affirm God's love for you and your commitment to diligence and excellence in your endeavors. Being a good steward of what God's entrusted to you- time, money, and opportunities- should be your focus instead of 'getting rich.' *"Seek ye first the Kingdom of God and His righteousness, and ALL these things shall be added unto you."* — Matthew 6:33

Fifth, take action: your faith in God must be exercised to be strengthened. In the book of James it says *"faith without works is dead."* Two strategies that will supercharge your results seizing the opportunities outlined in the next few chapters of this book are building a MasterMind team of advisors and creating key strategic partnerships.

A MasterMind, as outlined by Napoleon Hill, is a meeting of the minds where the combined energy of several minds towards solving challenges is greater than the sum of its parts. So if you have 3 people brainstorming a solution together in unison, you might be able to harness the equivalent *"brainpower"* of 5 or 10 people because you're acting in harmony. Many people think Napoleon Hill was the first person to expound on the MasterMind principle, but he wasn't. The first was actually King Solomon when he wrote *"Plans fail for lack of counsel, but with many advisers they succeed."* For even greater evidence of how important MasterMinds are, consider these 2 proverbs: *"There is a way that seems right to a man, but in the end it leads to death"* and *"With many counselors victory is assured."*

If you struggle with receiving advice from others, beware the dire consequences ahead and humble yourself enough to accept others' input! When you do, God will bless you.

Creating key strategic partnerships follows the same *"safety in numbers"* theme. It's based on Ecclesiastes 3:9-10&12, which states, *"Two are better than one, because they have a good return for their labor: if either of them falls down, one can help the other up. Though one may be overpowered, two can defend themselves. A cord of three strands is not quickly broken."* These verses show that for maximum profit in your endeavors, you should have at least one if not multiple strategic partners working alongside you.

It's very important to have discernment when picking MasterMind and strategic partners. The key elements the people that you consider should possess are the following: 1. they should be God-fearing and honest, 2. they should believe in you and be willing to offer support and advice, and 3. ideally, they should have skills and strengths that complement yours. You want to compensate for each others' weaknesses, not have 2 or 3 clones with all the same strengths and weaknesses.

So, are we in agreement that conventional wisdom stinks? Following it guarantees 90% of you will be retiring in mediocrity, leaving many of your life's dreams unfulfilled.

Are we also in agreement that there are different sets of *"truths"* out there and that you can choose to believe God's truth? Good. Isn't it great to know if you grew up poor or middle class you can choose to adopt the mindset of prosperous people in order to become prosperous? Praise God for that!

To get more in-depth training on picking good MasterMind partners, mentors, and strategic partners, read *"The Richest Man Who Ever Lived"* by Steven K. Scott and get his course *"Master Strategies of Super Achievers."*

Now that you know that most of us were taught a formula for financial failure, use the exercises below to identify and NOW replace those limiting beliefs with God's truth!

PRACTICAL EXERCISES FOR THIS CHAPTER:

(Fill in your dreams here! Don't be afraid to dream big and be disappointed- if you shoot for the moon you just may end up among the stars.)

Write Out Your Dream Lifestyle (where you live, the car you drive, what you do with your time, who you help, what your desired multi-generational legacy looks like - be as specific as possible, and write out your vision in the present tense, i.e. "*I live in... I drive... Four hours/week, I help...*" etc.):

_____
_____
_____
_____
_____
_____
_____
_____
_____
_____
_____
_____
_____

Read this every night before you go to bed and visualize living this lifestyle in as much detail as possible. This technique is called Psycho-Cybernetics and has been used by over 30 million people to change their lives.

Exercise: Improve YOUR Money Blueprint Write your CURRENT beliefs about money & prosperity.. Be honest about limiting beliefs.

Write your NEW ways of thinking about prosperity and handling money, health, and relationships - your new blueprint

- Write them as affirmations including Bible verses to reinforce the affirmations' truth.

_____
_____
_____
_____
_____
_____
_____
_____
_____
_____

Read your new Prosperity Blueprint and Dream Lifestyle out loud when you wake in the morning and go to bed at night. Changing your beliefs is your first step on your journey to becoming prosperous. Do these verbal exercises daily for the next 30+ days, and see what a difference they make!

CHAPTER 2

"Something's Wrong With the World Today..."

If you just completed the exercise at the end of the last chapter, congratulations! If you didn't, I encourage you to go back now and spend 10-15 minutes to fill it out; it will be one of the best time investments you make in your family's financial well-being. And it will help you deal with what I'm about to reveal to you in this chapter much more powerfully.

As I said earlier, I'm about to reveal a big crisis to you... and I want you to see that as a good thing for you because you're reading this book. For those who are unprepared for it, it will be very dangerous indeed.

In 1992, Aerosmith released a song called *"Living on the Edge"* with the opening lines *"Something's wrong with the world today. I don't know what it is. Something's wrong with our eyes. We're seeing things in a different way n' God knows it ain't His. Sure ain't no surprise. We're living on the edge."*

When it comes to the world's finances, there's DEFINITELY something wrong and we're living on the edge of disaster. Don't take my word for it- see what the official statistics are according to the world's financial experts:

- Inflation is rampant. In many countries it hovers around 6-10% or more. In the past year, commodity prices have jumped 18-20% which you've probably already noticed as your grocery bill has gone up considerably.

- The sovereign debt levels of many nations are unsustainable. Although the debt crises of Greece and Ireland have grabbed the most headlines in the past year, the U.S. has the biggest problem with $120.8 Trillion in unfunded liabilities according to the U.S. Federal Reserve. This amounts to over$398K/American, and the average American is only worth $50K. This affects you because most commodity prices like oil are measured in U.S.

dollars. A collapsing dollar means higher prices for you at the pump.

- World leaders COULD cut entitlements in half and slash spending to stabilize their currencies (like U.K. leaders recently did- congrats to them), but many of them went in the opposite direction- they put MORE money in the system and raised spending!! The U.S. alone is running $1.5Trillion/year deficits (over PHP50 Trillion/year!), and even China did almost $1Trillion in deficit spending in 2009/2010. So, what does it all add up to? Most world currencies will keep losing value, and some of them may even collapse soon.

- As many central banks are flooding the world with new paper money, we're likely headed for big-time inflation in the next few years. This robs money from savers of cash. For example, if today PHP50 buys you a loaf of bread and next week it takes PHP60 to buy the same loaf of bread, you're less motivated to save money because it's losing its purchasing power so quickly.

Are most countries' currencies going to recover once this recession is over? How likely are these trends to seriously affect you? What should you do to protect yourself from all of these risks? Are you fine keeping your cash in Philippine pesos, or should you diversify part of your wealth to other currencies and/or gold and silver?

To help answer these important questions, let's take a look at the history of money to give us a more complete perspective on what we're facing now.

What exactly is money anyway?

First, it's important to clarify what the difference is between money and currency. If you're like most people you haven't had anyone take the time to explain the difference, so please allow me to do so.

Currency is a medium of exchange people use to do transactions together. It started off with trading livestock and milk for rice and mangoes, and trading caribous for chickens and pigs became difficult as people created more kinds of goods, and technology enabled traveling further.

Eventually people needed something more portable, so metal coins and then paper currency were created. Today with credit cards, you can carry $1.5M USD or more (PHP 75,000,000+) on an American Express black card 2"x3" in size.

Money is anything that has real tangible value. Throughout all of history, money has been gold and silver. As early as the 2nd chapter of Genesis in the Bible, gold was considered rare, and was valued because of its rarity. Only in the last few hundred years has paper currency replaced gold and silver coins as the kind of money people carry with them.

So, money is always more valuable than currency because it can't be devalued by printing more of it. There's only so much gold and silver above ground, and the amount of gold mined every year equals only 1% of the existing world supply of it.

Why Fiat Currencies Collapse

Throughout history, every fiat currency ever created has collapsed. EVERY one. Why? Before I tell you why, let's define what a fiat currency is.

At the beginning, countries start with sound currency, meaning their currency is backed by gold. Governments and politicians want to please their people, so as their nations prosper they give their people more services. When they have a recession, or some war to fund they can't afford, they don't have the guts to reduce their services and risk facing the wrath of their subjects or not getting re-elected.

Instead, they spend more than they make and "*create*" more currency than they have gold to redeem, thus diluting and devaluing their existing currency. When a currency is fiat, it's value is not based upon gold - i.e. real money- it's only value is whatever the government says it is, and at that point (due to human nature) every fiat currency is doomed to be worthless.

There have been hundreds of fiat currencies in the past 2500 years, and every one has failed.

As a first example, let's review what happened in Rome in the 290s; Gaius became Emperor during a time of rampant inflation. Rome had weakened the value of their currency a lot by first nicking the edge of coins off as a tax when citizens paid for things, then by adding copper to their gold and silver coins. Eventually their currency had almost no gold in them and became worth little because people wouldn't spend their original gold coins to buy anything and prices were going up so fast.

To try and stop inflation, Gaius declared the Edict of Prices in 301 freezing wages and making it illegal to sell goods above their current prices. Despite his Edict, prices kept rising and eventually many farmers and shop owners stopped selling their goods because they couldn't make a profit. This led to things getting even MORE expensive and created the world's first documented hyperinflation.

Eventually Rome's currency collapsed. In 301 AD, 1 pound of gold cost 50,000 denari. By 350 AD, 1 pound of gold cost 2.12 billion denari. This equates to the price of gold going up 42,400 times.

To put this in perspective, in the 1950s 1 oz of gold cost $35 in the U.S. If it rose 42,400 times it would cost almost $1.5 Million per ounce. In terms of purchasing power, as the average car cost $2,000 in the 1950s, with 42,400 times inflation that car would cost $87.5 Million today. Imagine a Honda costing $80M USD (PHP 4 Billion) today! Crazy, yes? So, would you want to have held denari or gold during those years? Of course, you'd want gold.

Lest you think *"that was then and a hyperinflation can't happen here"* let me give you a very recent nearby example. On December 3, 2009, overnight Kim Jong Il devalued his currency by 10,000%. That means that if a North Korean citizen had 100,000 won on December 3, on December 4 they could only exchange their old currency for 1,000 won. Talk about government theft!

As the PI economy is developing rapidly, lest you think a hyperinflation can't happen in a modern, developed economy, I have one last example to share with you.

In 1918 at the end of WWI, Germany's citizens started spending again as they had saved almost all their money during the war as people do in times of uncertainty. Although they had no inflation during the war, Germany had gone off the gold standard at the start of the war- i.e. went fiat- and had printed 400% more German Marks during the war. Here's how inflation showed up in the next 5 years...

Date:	German Marks needed to buy one ounce of gold
Jan 1919	170.00
Sept 1919	499.00
Jan 1920	1,340.00
Sept 1920	1,201.00
Jan 1921	1,349.00
Sept 1921	2,175.00
Jan 1922	3,976.00
Sept 1922	30,381.00
Jan 1923	372,477.00
Sept 1923	269,439,000.00
Oct 2, 1923	6,631,749,000.00
Oct 9, 1923	24,868,950,000.00
Oct 16, 1923	84,969,072,000.00
Oct 23, 1923	1,160,552,882,000.00
Oct 30, 1923	1,347,070,000,000.00
Nov 5, 1923	8,700,000,000,000.00
Nov 30, 1923	87,000,000,000,000.00

Just before the end of WWI, 1 oz of gold only cost 100 Marks. At the end of the war and 5 years later it cost 87 TRILLION Marks. To show you that hyperinflation can be sneaky, notice in the chart that throughout 1920 gold only cost 1000-2000 Marks. So prices rose 10-20 times and stabilized for 1.5 years.

After gold broke past 2000 Marks in Sept. 1921, hyperinflation started to show up. In one year from Sept. 1921 to Sept. 1922, prices rose over 10 times, and from Sept. 1922 to Sept. 1923 prices rose almost 100,000 times.

Gold wasn't the only thing whose price was exploding. By November 1923, an egg went from .08 Marks to 80 Billion Marks, and a loaf of bread went from half a Mark to 200 Billion Marks. In the whole German economy only gold and silver's value rose faster than the rate of inflation. How did this happen so fast? The people lost confidence in their currency by the summer of 1922, when prices on most goods rose another 700 percent in under 1 year. When people lose confidence in their currency, they spend it as soon as they get it, because they know it won't buy tomorrow what it buys today. The picture on this page graphically illustrates how truly worthless fiat currency is!

German children play with a pile of Deutsche Marks

Today central banks all over the world are doing the same thing and working their printing presses overtime to print more currency. You'd be foolish to think it won't end up in a hyperinflation in your country sooner or later (probably sooner).

So, is it inevitable that your government (or someone else's government) will always rob the purchasing power of your pesos and dollars? No, it's not. Through most of recent history, paper currency was backed by gold or silver coin - i.e. *"real money."*

For example, through 1933 you could go to any U.S. bank and exchange your paper currency for real money because it said right on the bills *"redeemable for gold & silver coin."*

When governments control their spending and keep taxes low, it's easy for them to have their currency backed by gold money and there often is little or no inflation. An example of this is that, from approximately 1500 to 1700, in the country of England, there was NO inflation at all.

To show how powerful this is, imagine things costing the same amount today as they did when you were a kid. Imagine a Coke only costing 5 or 10 Centavos today. That's what it was like in England for 5 generations straight! The fact that this idea boggles your mind or amazes you shows you how much we have lowered our expectations of our governments to control their spending and maintain ample money reserves to back up our currencies.

How ALL Currencies Became Fiat

In 1944 towards the end of WWII, representatives from 44 countries met in Bretton Woods, NH, and the world leaders agreed to have the U.S. dollar back up all other currencies because the U.S. held most of the world's gold at the end of the war. This had a few main effects. First, it made all the other currencies of the world dependent on the U.S. dollar, and commodities became priced in dollars. The other effect it had is it gave the U.S. unprecedented power to run massive deficits and print new currency because other central banks around the world had to hold a percentage of their reserves in U.S. dollars.

In the late 1960s, France found a loophole in the Bretton Woods agreement and began redeeming many of their U.S. dollars for gold. At the same time the Vietnam War was costing the U.S. a lot of money and other nations started redeeming their dollars for gold too.

Gold was leaving the U.S. so fast that then President Richard Nixon did a very drastic thing- without consulting Congress or the State Dept. he took the U.S. off the gold standard - meaning he broke the Bretton Woods agreement - and the U.S. no longer needed to have a percentage of their currency in circulation backed by real gold money.

When Nixon took the global reserve currency off the gold standard in 1971, he made ALL the currencies of the world (including the Philippine Peso) into fiat currencies instantly with one stroke of the pen. Crazy, right?!?

Since then, the U.S. dollar has no longer been backed by gold and the number of dollars in circulation has increased by 3000+%. Also, inflation has been rising at higher and higher amounts globally in the past few decades.

Where will these trends take us next? Let's look to history to give us the answer.

How to Get Back to Real Money, and What to Do in the Meantime

So what happens when things get really *"out of whack"* with printed fiat currencies, and inflation grows faster as in the Germany, Rome, and North Korea examples we highlighted?

First, the price of gold revalues to account for all the printed currency in circulation. In the U.S. alone, this happened twice in the past 80 years- most recently in 1980 when gold rose to $825/oz and silver rose to just over $51/oz. Amazingly, even though the amount of U.S. currency and credit had grown by over 200% from Bretton Woods through 1980, the U.S. could have gone back to the gold standard that year.

Lucky for you and me, they didn't. Your opportunity to profit mightily lives on!

This also happened in 1933 after FDR made owning gold privately illegal and issued an Executive Order demanding all U.S. citizens exchange their gold for dollars. Don't fear the government making it illegal for you to own gold today; even back in 1933 only 22% of people turned in their gold, and no one who broke the *"gold hoarding"* law was ever prosecuted or even arrested.

The 78% of U.S. citizens who broke the law were smart. Why? Because in 9 months the price of gold went from $20/oz to $35/oz. Basically the dollar lost 69% of its value in 1 year.

So, those that turned in their gold lost 70% of their purchasing power in one year, and those that didn't increased their purchasing power 70% at the same time. This goes to show you that you must take responsibility to grow your wealth and not depend on the government.

When spending gets too out of control, they ALWAYS fail eventually. When they fail, the government creates a new currency once again backed by gold and silver in their reserves.

Remember that due to to all currencies being fiat today and recent large inflation, many of the currencies of the world will likely fail in the coming years. It could be in 2 years or it could be in 5-10 years. Only the Lord knows the future and I'm not a psychic. But what I do know is that EVERY fiat currency in the history of the world has failed eventually, and there's no reason to think this time it will be any different.

So, how much gold and silver should you buy? When should you buy? Is it too late to buy as gold has gone from $300/oz in 2000 to over $2000/oz in 2023? In what form and from where should you buy your gold and silver? When should you sell it, and to whom?

These are all great questions, and it's important you get the right answers to them all. We'll cover the key things you need to know about buying gold and silver in the next chapter, and when and how to safely sell your gold and silver afterwards.

In the meantime, I want to share a strategy with you that you won't read in any other books about protecting your wealth with investments in gold and silver: prayer.

In the book *"Shaping History Through Prayer and Fasting,"* the author reveals how he fasted and prayed for over 2 years that the Lord would bring a righteous commander to his unit that was fighting in North Africa in WWII. The Lord heard his prayers, and moved on his behalf mightily! The book shares many amazing stories of God's provision and reveals many specific strategies you can use to change the world with prayer.

I strongly encourage you to pray daily for righteous leaders to rule justly. Pray for your current Philippines leaders (from the President all the way down to your local barangay captain) that God will give them wisdom to rule justly, to limit spending, and to keep ample gold reserves in the BSP (Banko Sentral ng Pilipinas ie the PI central bank).

During election cycles pray for the Lord to raise up righteous leaders, and don't complain about things politicians do unless you're praying for them daily. Your prayers will make a big difference in the Philippines, so be diligent in your prayers in faith. *"The prayers of a righteous man avails much"* – James 5:16

When the coming currency collapses arrive, most will be unprepared and will have their wealth wiped out. The poor will remain poor and many rich people that have wise advisors will be able to preserve their wealth. You have this book, so you'll be ready!

Let's dive into the best ways for you to buy gold and silver for your family's financial well-being...

CHAPTER 3

All That Glitters Isn't Gold

In the last chapter, we covered the difference between money and currency, historic examples of inflation and what people who bought precious metals were able to accomplish, and established that there's no escaping the devaluation of the Philippine peso, U.S. dollar, and other currencies as they are all fiat currencies as of 1971.

As you've discovered, owning gold and silver is the best way to protect yourselves in times of large inflation. We'll cover when, how, and how much you should buy in this chapter, and when and how to sell in the next chapter.

As the title of this chapter states, not all ways to buy gold and silver are equal. To the contrary, many of the ways to own gold and silver that are marketed in the media don't give you enough control or profit potential to make it an attractive investment.

Before we jump in to very specific strategies, let me point out one very key point. The goal when buying gold and silver is not to own it. Sure, it looks pretty but it doesn't create cashflow and you can't do much with it.

The goal is to buy it in highly inflationary times, and then be able to sell it when things settle down to buy lots of assets that will pay you income. Remember the German example of buying a block of commercial real estate for 25 oz of gold? That's what you're aiming for!

In the last chapter on page 52, I posed several questions about if it's too late to buy gold and silver as their price has gone up so much in the past 5-10 years. Those are fair questions. To get the answers, let's look at the historic price cycles that most assets go through.

Are You Ready for a Wild Ride?

I love rollercoasters. It's quite a thrill to fly down a 90° hill at 150Km/hr and to fly around sharp curves feeling the G-forces on your body. Most markets are like rollercoasters in that their prices are always going up or down cyclically. Whether it's stocks, rice, the Peso, or gold, the patterns are very similar (though they usually don't go straight down).

Most markets go through similar phases in their cycles of going up and down. The phases are as follows:

<u>Seller Phase 1</u> — the price of an asset reaches a bottom and starts to rise. The savviest investors are able to buy it in this phase.

<u>Seller Phase 2</u> — an asset's price rises a little faster as more investors buy it.

<u>Seller Phase 3</u> — an asset's price rises further and average investors become aware of its' valuation. Only 5-10% of investors buy it.

<u>Seller Phase 4</u> — an asset's price rises very suddenly when the masses buy in. Often a bubble- a large spike up in price in a short time- is formed at the end of this phase.

<u>Buyer Phase 1</u> — the price of an asset reaches a top and starts to fall. The savviest investors sell in this phase. Often the price falls suddenly because savvy investors hold large positions in the asset, but average investors hold on to it.

Buyer Phase 2 — an asset's price falls further, but not as quickly as in Seller Phase 1. Many smart investors sell at this phase.

Buyer Phase 3 — an asset's price continues to fall, and some average investors sell at this point.

Buyer Phase 4 — an asset's price falls a little more and starts to flatten out. Disgusted, most average investors sell at a big loss and vow not to "*buy (asset's name) again.*"

The first 4 phases are called Seller phases because when an asset's price is rising sellers ask for a higher price and usually get it. This is also known as a "*seller's market.*"

The last 4 phases are called Buyer phases for the opposite reason; prices are falling, so buyers can offer a lower price and usually get it. This is also known as a "*buyer's market.*"

So, back to whether it's too late for you to buy gold and silver for yourself. There are 2 pieces of good news for you:

1. at the time of this writing, we're only in a Seller Phase 3 market, which the prices of gold and silver both have a lot of upside potential.

2. The even BETTER news is that only about 1% of investors are buying gold and silver, and of those

investors probably only 10% of them are buying the metals the right way.

So that means even though gold has gone from $300/oz in 2000 to $1500+/oz and silver has gone up a lot the past 10 years also, there's still a lot of profits to be made.

In addition to those two factors, when gold accounts for all the currency in circulation today it should go to $5000/oz minimum (cash expansion) up to $26,000+/oz (cash + credit expansion). So there's still a lot of potential profit in both gold and silver if you move fast.

As both markets still have yet to enter buyer phase 4, I think you should buy both ASAP.

Let me stress again that the biggest reason to buy gold and silver for yourself is to protect your wealth from being wiped out, not to make 100% to 500% return on your money. Increasing the value of your wealth is the target vs. just raising the amount of your net worth. (more on that in a little bit)

Given all these timing factors, I recommend you buy gold and silver for yourself ASAP as long as we remain in a Seller Phase 3 market for them both. Once we enter a Seller Phase 4 market, you should be very careful about making sure you don't buy them at their peak price only to have them drop a lot right after you buy them. **How do you know when we're near a top in price?** Let me tell you a story that will illustrate it perfectly:

From 1972 to June 1979, you could have bought gold from $100 to $200/oz. (Seller Phases 2 and 3; it went from $35 to $100/oz in 1971- Seller Phase 1). It was only from July 1979 to January 1980 that gold went from $200 to $895/oz. (Seller Phase 4).

It was during fall/winter 1979 that you saw lines a block long outside of gold coin shops. When there's a buying frenzy, you start to see lines of people outside stores, and everyone including non-investors are talking about an asset, then know that the top in price is near.

By the way, if you bought in Seller Phases 1- 3, you would have had a lot of time to sell your gold at $600+ before it fell sharply as well. If you had bought gold in 1971 outside the U.S. at $35/oz you could have easily made 20x your money, or 2000% ROI.

How Should You Invest in Gold & Silver?

There are many ways to buy gold and silver, and as I said at the beginning of this chapter most of them leave you without control. I suggest you ONLY hold your gold and silver one of 2 ways: in bullion coins and bars in your physical possession and in your own segregated storage vault. In a moment I'm going to tell you the best places to buy your gold and silver, but first let's quickly review why you don't want to buy gold or silver the other ways they are commonly marketed.

Gold or Silver Certificates: You should avoid these because you can't verify that the gold your certificates are for is actually in the vault or the bank, and often the same certificates are sold to multiple investors as a scam. Even banks have been caught selling certificates for gold that they didn't have in their possession.

Collective storage vaults: There are several vaults in Asia, Europe, and America that store hundreds and hundreds of billions worth of gold bullion bars and coins for investors. If you put your gold and silver in a vault like this, it can easily get mixed up with someone else's. Stick with a segregated account where your metal is separated from other peoples'.

Numismatics/collector coins: There are two reasons why you should never buy these as an investment. First, they are commonly forged and counterfeited and then sold for 8-10 times what they are worth. Don't fall victim to them. Second, in times of crisis like hyper- inflation, the value of real numismatic coins falls to their value in bullion. Imagine you buy a collector silver coin for $800 (PHP 40,000) when silver bullion sells for $30/oz (PHP 1500/oz). Three years later there's hyperinflation and silver goes to $300/oz (PHP 15,000/oz). Those who bought bullion made a 10X return, yet you've lost $500 (PHP 25,000). Buy numismatics as a collector, and stick to bullion for investing.

What Coins I Recommend to Buy and Why

It will be awesome when Filipinos are so wealthy that the BSP can start making its own gold and silver bullion coins, but for now no such coins exist; that's why I recommend you buy gold and silver American Eagle bullion coins for 2 main reasons. First, the U.S. and the Philippines have a special relationship so there's no duty or taxes to pay buying or selling bullion coins from America. Second, American Eagles are the most widely recognized and traded bullion coins in the world, so they're easy to buy and sell.

The best place to buy your American Eagle coins is **GoldSilver.com**. They allow you to buy the smallest amount of metal of almost any coin broker (20 Silver Eagles or 1 Gold Eagle minimum vs. 70 Silver Eagles minimum order at Kitco.com), and they'll ship your bullion to your door internationally insured via UPS/DHL/FedEx very discreetly. The package will come from "*GSI*" so even your delivery man won't know what it is.

If you have a connection to a local coin dealer in the PI and they can get you coins locally at a fair price, go for it. I haven't found one yet, and at Sulit. com.ph the cheapest silver bullion coin I found today was PHP3500- almost double the bullion price- with 1 available.

Here are the BENEFITS of buying gold and silver bullion the ways I recommend:

Bullion in your Possession: when you have gold and silver in your possession, it's easy to access and to use in time of crisis. Also, bullion coins are easy to verify as legitimate when it comes time to sell them. I recommend only you and your spouse know where you keep them. Don't tell your relatives or kids as there will be too much temptation to talk. With your metals, silence is golden.

For when you take physical delivery of your gold and silver coins, on the following pages are pictures of what they look like so you can tell the real thing from a counterfeit. ☺ ⇨

American Eagle GOLD One Ounce Bullion Coin

American Eagle SILVER One Ounce Bullion Coin

Plastic Containers of 20 Eagle Coins Each from the U.S. Mint (says *"US Treasury"* on lid)

Box of 500 SILVER American Eagle Coins from the U.S. Mint- a box of 500 coins (either GOLD or SILVER) will always have the two seals on it with the name of the mint the coins were made at. In this case, the coins were minted in West Point, Virginia. *Without the seals, assume the box has been opened and check each container inside.

Segregated Vault Storage: if you're going to buy $20,000 (PHP1,000,000) or more of gold and silver coins, for convenience and safety you may want to store some of it in a vault. It's up to your comfort level. With segregated vault storage, you don't have to worry about storing your metals, and your metals are separated from others' metals. GoldSilver.com has vault storage available in the U.S. and Europe.

How Much Gold/Silver Should You Buy?

I'm going to answer this question 2 ways: first, as a breakdown of what % of your metals are gold and what % is silver, and then as a % of your overall net worth.

First, I recommend 90% of your metal holdings should be silver and 10% of it should be gold. I recommend this for several reasons:

1. Silver is much cheaper than gold so it's easier to buy in lots of $800 or so.

2. Silver is much easier to use for small purchases in times of crisis. You don't want to use a $2,000 gold coin to buy groceries.

3. Silver has more profit potential than gold. For the first time in recorded history, there's less silver above ground than gold. This is because almost all gold is stored as money with only 1% being used for industry. Silver is the #2 most-used industrial commodity after petroleum, and the expanded sales of electronics it's used in, means demand for it will only grow. This means silver will become rarer and rarer, which should push its price up significantly in the coming years.

So, if you have $20,000 (PHP1,000,000), put $18,000 (PHP900K) into silver and put $2,000 (PHP100K) into gold.

As far as what % of your net worth should be put into precious metals, first a disclaimer: I'm not a financial planner, nor do I play one on TV. You should always consult with your team of experts- lawyers, accountants, financial advisors, and your MasterMind team- when making any major decisions. So I'm not going to tell you what you should do.

However, I WILL tell you what King Solomon recommends you do with your wealth and how I would model his wisdom in different scenarios.

In Ecclesiastes 11:2, King Solomon advises *"Divide your portion to seven, or even to eight, for you do not know what misfortune may occur on the earth."*

How I apply Solomon's wisdom is to invest in the following: personal coaching, business coaching, growing my business, commercial real estate (apartments), and precious metals. I own 5 different companies, so that works out to 8 or 9 things I divide my time and money portion into that God has entrusted to me.

No matter what you do for work- whether you're a worker, business owner, investor, or a combination of the 3- I recommend you invest regularly in yourself with coaching and training. I invest about 10% of my business profits in growing myself, and that's resulted in me working on $100M+ projects. I don't tell you that to impress you as it's only by the grace of God; I tell you that to demonstrate the power of this principle when you apply it.

Ben Franklin said *"Empty your mind to fill your pockets, and your pockets will fill your mind continually."* You're reading this book, so keep up the good work. I've found the key to getting the biggest profit from your investment in yourself is to make the gap between when you learn something new and when you implement it as short as possible. Wealth is very attracted to those who take wise, decisive action.

I also apply Solomon's wisdom by looking for passive income cashflow vehicles to invest in. My personal preference is apartment buildings, and yours may be franchises or other existing, well-run businesses you can buy. Find what's the best fit for you, because as you grow your wealth quickly with precious metals you're going to need something to invest your windfall profits into.

Lastly, it's always wise to leave some cash on-hand. You may want to consider putting ½ of your cash on-hand into precious metals and depending on how much you have left perhaps hold one other currency in addition to US Dollars, Euros, and Philippine Pesos. These days, I'd rather hold a mixture of different currencies than US dollars alone, but that's just my preference. In the next chapter, we cover how to further diversify your holdings into digital dollars and digital gold to protect your wealth.

If you currently own a portfolio of stocks or land that's undeveloped, I'd strongly consider selling it and putting the money into precious metals. Here's why: let's say you have PHP1,000,000 in the PI stock market and over the next 3 years it doubles. Great, right? But what if in the same 3 years a Peso buys half of what it did today? You wouldn't be ahead by a single Centavo. This is a very real inflation risk considering all the factors we've covered so far, so be wise! Consider converting at least PART of your holdings to bullion.

I would even consider selling part of your holdings if your family owns some heirloom gold and silver buried out in the woods, and convert it to gold and silver bullion. Here's why: in a panic when currencies collapse, people are trying to get rid of paper currency as fast as possible.

If God-forbid there's a major collapse of the Philippine Peso, the last thing you want to be trying to do is get your metals assayed to verify their purity just so you can exchange some of it for food or a car or whatever you're buying. Convert it to bullion ASAP so you'll be able to use it easily in times of turmoil. As in all things, prepare for the worst and hope for the best. Just don't get caught unprepared!

I want to end this chapter by emphasizing the fact that much more important than the PRICE you can buy and sell gold and silver at, you should focus on the VALUE you can get for it in the next few years.

For example, in Germany at the end of WWI in 1918, 1 oz of gold sold for 100 German Marks. As the graph on page 45 shows, by 1920, 1 oz of gold was worth 1,000 to 2,000 Marks. Retail prices quickly followed, jumping 10-20 times. Just think- what if gas went from PHP50/litre to PHP500 - PHP1000/litre in the next year? In a hyperinflation, that's what happens.

By the end of 1923, it took 87 TRILLION Marks to buy 1 oz. of gold. A pair of shoes that cost 12 Marks in 1918 cost 20 Trillion Marks by the end of 1923! Simply replace Marks with Pesos, and imagine you had PHP100,000 in September 1920 as your life's savings.

If you left it in cash, your purchasing power was reduced to a tank of gas in only 3 years. If you converted it to gold as late as September 1921, you could buy 50 oz of gold with your wealth. What could that buy you?

At the end of 1923, you could buy a whole block of commercial real estate in downtown Berlin for 25 oz of gold, so if you were savvy and converted your money to gold consistently with your savings, you could have bought 2 whole city blocks of commercial real estate with your original $20,000 (PHP100,000) when the things settled down!

So, the GOOD news is that you can come out of a hyperinflation VERY wealthy even if you're middle class to start, as long as you act wisely. If you follow the sheeple (the uninformed masses), you'll get sheared and have your wealth wiped out.

I trust that by looking in-depth into the 1920s Germany example, you are now motivated to buy some gold and silver bullion coins as long as we're still in a Seller Phase 3 market for precious metals. Go for the gold!

CHAPTER 4

Protect Yourself from the WEF Agenda 2030 & Other Threats

If you're a lover of freedom, this chapter will help you financially survive and thrive now... and in the days ahead when tyranny will likely increase globally.

This chapter will show you how to protect yourself from growing threats to your wealth, from bank crashes to the inflation we're seeing all over the globe. On top of that, the WEF's Agenda 2030 of *"you're going to own nothing and be happy"* by the year 2030 is a big threat to you also. The three US banks that were closed in spring 2023, including the 3rd largest bank failure in US history of Silicon

Valley Bank, are very likely tied to the United States government's attempt to control crypto. There's a banking contagion happening all over the globe with UBS merging with Credit Suisse in Switzerland spring '23, and more banks are at risk of failing now.

Pro Tip: To best honor your time, I encourage you to take notes while you go through this chapter, as you think of specific actions you should take to now protect your wealth. The purpose of this chapter is to empower you with strategies that will help you not only survive the uncertainty of what is happening right now, but even to maintain your wealth and grow your wealth in the midst of what we're dealing with now.

So let's get right into it. First of all, I'm not a lawyer or CPA, nor do I play one on TV. I HAVE published 3 books, and I've been interviewed on television, radio, and podcasts all over the world- in the USA, Philippines, Europe, Africa, and Dubai. Everything I share here is based upon King Solomon's trainings and teachings in the books of Proverbs and Ecclesiastes, in what Jews call the Torah and Christians call the Bible. As always, consult your financial and legal advisors when considering implementing any financial strategies.

What most people don't realize is that King Solomon was a very innovative businessperson, and **he created a $4 trillion** fortune using his wisdom principles to build a business. I'm going to share with you some of his key wisdom principles that apply to the season that we're in right now, and how you can use Solomon's wisdom to maximize your results financially.

Also, I've also been able to talk to 122 billionaires (22 of them one-on-one), including David Green, founder of Hobby Lobby, Chris Larsen that co-founded Ripple/XRP, and Brock Pierce, co-creator of USDT/Tether. David Green said I help people maximize their legacy and their plans for their family, and I plan to support YOU and YOUR legacy with this timely chapter.

So let's jump right into it. What are some principles of Solomon that you can apply right now that are most appropriate for applying in the situation that we're in right now globally? I'm going to share with you four of his teachings that I think are really, really key to apply right now.

Number one, "*a wise person sees danger and takes precaution; a fool keeps going and they suffer for it.*" Do not be a fool and suffer. Look at what's going on, and take the proper precautions. That's what this chapter will help you do.

Number two, *"in the house of the wise are many beautiful treasures, and wealth is not secured for future generations."* Whether you're worth $500K, you're worth a million, or you're worth a billion while reading this, it's vital that you protect your wealth; it's not guaranteed that that wealth will stay in your family.

Thirdly, right now we need next-level wisdom and knowledge and understanding. There are multiple proverbs that say, *"with all thy getting, get knowledge, get understanding, get wisdom."* In this chapter, I'm going to share with you some knowledge you might not know. Maybe you already know 80% of what I'll share today; I'll share with you some new knowledge, some understanding of what's going on and how to apply that knowledge, and then wisdom would be you taking massive action. Implement this chapter's strategies to help protect yourself, and get the benefits that come from taking powerful, strategic actions.

Last but not least, almost all of modern financial planning is based upon this teaching of Solomon which comes out of the book of Ecclesiastes, which says, *"divide your portion into seven or eight for you do not know what misfortune may happen on the Earth.*" We're seeing a lot of misfortune right now. Back in 2008 we saw it. Before that in 2001 we saw misfortune on 9/11 and many times before that. Now we must adjust to THIS economic cycle's risks.

There are actually bigger risks with banking right now than there were in 2008, because the 2008 crisis was strictly related to mortgage over-lending in the United States. The reason why is that since COVID lockdowns began, central banks ALL over the world have been printing money like crazy; inflation is growing and it's a global problem... so you need next-level strategy.

Let me share with you some strategies that I recommend you implement ASAP, and I encourage you lastly, ask God for wisdom about how you should best implement the strategies I'm going to share with you now.

Okay, so number one, before we get into the four strategies, I want to encourage you that gold is really important. If you don't realize it, central banks around the world for the last year have been buying record amounts of gold. Up until 1971, all money in the world was backed by gold, and many central banks realize money needs to be backed by gold again in order to be stable and address growing worldwide inflation.

One thing I learned from a multimillionaire mentor is to follow the elephant tracks, which means look and see what the biggest investors are doing, and model them. Central banks are the biggest investors in the world, and they are buying lots of gold. As central banks are buying gold like crazy, you should be buying gold as well.

Protection Strategy #1:

Reduce your banking risk.

I just heard this shocking data recently from a friend of mine who works on Wall Street: an analyst that he works with says that up to 187 different banks in the United States are at risk of failing. That's the United States alone; the FDIC simply does not have enough cash.

You may have heard today that multiple tier two and midsize banks have been asking the FDIC to guarantee all of their depositors' savings, because what's happening is a lot of people are pulling their cash out of small banks, and putting them in the in the big 5 *"too big to fail"* banks.

I don't think it's healthy for us to have a lot more small banks close. It's important that we have a variety of options to pick from in terms of who we bank with. That gives us freedom, and it makes it much harder for our government to control us. And all people of the world deserve freedom.

The strategy I recommend you implement right now, is to keep accounts with a minimum of two banks, and ideally don't keep much more than $250K in any one account. Do not do all your banking with one bank; if you have a business account and a personal account, but they're with the same bank, go open up a new business and personal account with another bank.

I would recommend have one account with one of the really big banks, the 5 that are considered too big to fail- BofA, Wells Fargo, Chase, PNC, Wells Fargo, and JP Morgan. I would have an account with one of those 5, because if there's any major meltdown with the banking sector, the government will likely save those banks before they save some small banks. So I would have one with them.

And I would also have one bank account with a small regional credit union. Credit unions are owned by the members; they're a lot less risky with the clients funds. Last but not least, Warren Buffett calls derivatives weapons of mass financial destruction. If you have an account with the big banks, Google *"amount of derivatives (bank name), (country)"* to find out how much derivatives your bank has issued. You want to look for at least a 2 to 1 deposits versus derivatives ratio. Some banks have issued more derivatives then their total amounts of client deposits. So you want them to have double the deposits of their derivatives. That's an important insider tip at a high macro level.

Part of applying King Solomon's teaching "*divide your portion of the seven or eight*" would be to have your money in three different places. I recommend only have a third of your cash in the bank, a third in precious metals, and a third in physical cash. I'm going to give you the strategies for precious metals in a moment, and let's focus on best practices for holding cash.

Protection Strategy #2:

Keep your cash safe.

You need to buy a safe, that's waterproof and fireproof. You can find one for as little as $200 to $300; a 2 ft x 2 ft x 2 ft one is enough to store $100K to $200K. Two hundred thousand in hundreds is only 2000 bills, so it doesn't take up that much space. If you've ever withdrawn $2,000 from the bank, where they give you twenty $100 bills, then you know it doesn't take up that much space.

For up to $200K of cash and precious metals, a 2 ft x 2 ft x 2 ft safe is big enough. For $300K, get a safe that is 3 ft x 3 ft x 3 ft. And for $500K+ I recommend you get a gun safe. I personally have a waterproof and fireproof safe that's about 2.5 ft square, and it cost me under $400. They're very affordable for the safety they give. If you're going to save $500K to $1 Million dollars or more, it's worth it to spend a couple grand on a really good fireproof waterproof gun safe, and have an installer bolt it to the floor for you. I recommend you have it installed in a non- obvious place like in a basement, storage room, or big walk-in closet.

Only you, and your spouse or significant other, should know where your safe is. If you're single, only you need to know where it is. In your estate plan, write down where the safe is and the combination to open it. Put that information in a sealed letter with a trustee or your attorney, and when you pass away, your heirs know where to get that part of your estate. You don't want them to find a safe in your house and not know how to get into it.

Once you have your safe, the next thing to do is withdraw your cash from the bank. If you have $500K in the bank and you're taking out $150K or less (as that's a third of it), call your bank ahead of time and say, *"I want to withdraw $150,000 in cash; when can I come in to withdraw it?"* They might try to talk you out of it, and if they ask you why you're withdrawing so much cash, tell them you're diversifying your money to hedge against banking sector risk.

If they tell you they need any longer than a week to get that much cash together, ask them, "*I understand you need to get the cash together. How much can I withdraw within the next week?*" Let them tell you, "*Oh, you can take out $50K within a week*", or "*You can take out $100K five days from now.*" Sometimes if you ask for a larger amount of cash, they have to request the cash from their corporate office and it may take 2-4 weeks. Find out how much you can withdraw per week, while they request the larger amount of cash from their corporate office.

Banks have to write up these things called 'SAR's, or Suspicious Activity Reports. If they ask you why are you withdrawing the money, you don't want them to be suspicious; tell them directly, "*To hedge against banking sector risk and protect my family, I'm keeping some money in cash, and I'm putting some money in another bank. That's why I'm taking out the cash.*" That should be an ample answer that should not generate an SAR.

Be open with your banker about why you're withdrawing cash; don't be defensive and say, "*Why are you asking me this? It's my money and it's none of your business.*" Be an informed consumer and know that it's your banker's job to look for activities out of the ordinary. Calmly tell them what you're doing and why you're doing it, as it's perfectly logical to want to have some money in cash in case there's a big financial challenge. So that should be your answer.

If you have $100K in the bank, take out $35K to keep in cash, and take another $35K to put in metals (that's $70K total). One way to withdraw smaller amounts of cash is to go to your local bank, and take out $4500 to $4900 at a time 2-3 times/week.

Why I suggest $4500 is that many banks teach their tellers to look for patterns of multiple $5000+ withdrawals; if you do multiple $5K+ withdrawals, that will likely generate a SAR (Suspicious Activity Report). So just withdraw $4K to $4900 at a time, and if a bank teller ever asks about your withdrawals, tell them you're taking out some money to keep in cash, to hedge against banking sector risk and protect your family.

You can also take out the whole $70K at once. By all means, do call them and say, *"I want to withdraw 70 thousand cash next week; what day can I come and pick it up?"* Or you can withdraw $50K at once, and withdraw the other $20K in four to five different $4K to $4900 withdrawals while waiting for the cash to be sent to your local branch). So that's how you want to take your cash out of the bank.

Next, I suggest that you put a third of your liquid money into metals. In a moment, I'll show you how to buy metals with full privacy- without having to show your ID to the person that sells you the metals- this is why you want the third of your money that you're going to put into metals withdrawn from the bank into cash as well (and why I recommended above that you withdraw $70K per $100K you have in the bank into cash).

For withdrawing amounts over $60K, do bring a briefcase with you to the bank. You can buy the ones that have a lock code on them for $100, where you can lock the briefcase. Just so you know, $50K is only five hundred $100 bills, which can fit in 2-3 suit jacket pockets or winter jacket pockets; put two bands of $10K on one side and two on the other side, and the third $10K in a bottom pocket. You don't need a briefcase for $50K. To take out $100K I would say bring a briefcase, or you could do two different $50,000 withdrawals using a suit or purse.

If you plan to withdraw $200K or $300K from the bank in cash, like in the movies where they have the silver briefcase, then go to a branch that has a security guard and ask them to walk you to your car.

Another precaution to take is to make sure no one's following you during your drive home. And when you get home, put that money in your safe right away. Don't dilly dally; go right to your safe, open it up, put the cash in, and lock it. **Then you're going to get ready to buy your precious metals.**

One other last thing for if you have $1 Million to $20 Million + in the bank: I know a guy who literally had $53 million in the bank and the funds were frozen due to a false accusation from a local government official where he lived. Learn from his experience, and do not leave your money in the bank.

If he would have had $1 to $2 Million in cash and metals, he could have cleared his name and recouped his funds. So if you have $2 Million + in the bank, put $300K in cash, and put the other $300K (per $1M) in cash value of an insurance policy or T-bills.

Both universal index life and universal whole life insurance policies have cash value. You can read the books *"Become Your Own Banker"* or *"Bank On Yourself"* to learn more about the benefits and strategies of using these policies; in essence, you want a life insurance policy with a very small death benefit and a maxed out cash value, because the main purpose of your policy is to store a lot of cash in the cash value of the policy.

You can withdraw (borrow) against the cash value of your policy, just as you would withdraw funds from a bank. But unlike banks, who take your money and go and loan 10X the amount of your savings to other people, insurance companies do not loan out your money to other people. So this is why when you put $300K per $1M into the cash value of a life insurance policy, the annual premium would be very low because you have a small death benefit. So that's a couple of advanced strategies for bigger amounts of cash- T-bills and insurance policies.

It's vital you work with a life insurance agent who is knowledgeable about this strategy to BEST benefit from it. One guy I recommend is Matt Sapaula of PHP Agency. He's been a friend of mine going back over 15 years, and he has a team of people he's taught this strategy to across the United States. *Book a consultation with Matt's team at **https://livingmoneysmart.com/moneygame** and let them know David Roy Newby sent you! I also know three other insurance agents who are very well versed in this strategy, and know how to optimally set up one of those policies for you.

Protection Strategy #3:

Buy precious metals.

As we just talked about, you're going to take 2/3 of your cash out of the bank and use 1/3 of it (half of the cash) to buy precious metals. First, you're going to keep your metals in the fireproof waterproof safe that you bought to store your cash. **Second of all, you want to find a good local precious metals dealer near you.**

If you're in a rural area, and there is no precious metals dealer within an hour drive, then you can always buy gold on Kitco.com or GoldSilver.com. Whether you buy $10K or $100K+ of metals from them, they'll fully insure every package they ship to you.

For every $10K of metals you buy, you want to buy 80% Silver and 20% gold, and you want to buy Johnson Matthew bars, and American Eagle one ounce gold and silver coins..

Right now gold is around $2,000 per ounce. That means for every $10K, you'll buy one ounce of gold, which will be right around $2000, and then you buy the rest in silver Johnson Mathey 1 oz and 10 oz. bars and 1 oz American Eagle coins. (American Eagles are the most common 1 oz. coin in the world.)

One key reason to hold silver coins is this: if the power grid goes down for an extended period (like it did from NY to Michigan for 10 days in 2011), you can very easily trade silver for goods and services. Silver is around $25 an ounce, and gold is around $2,000 an ounce, so **it's a lot easier to buy $50 to $500 worth of stuff with some silver coins versus gold coins**. This is why you want to keep 80% in 1 to 10 oz. silver coins and silver bars, and 20% in gold coins.

For buying your metals, take $9,900 cash- removing one $100 bill from $10K wrapped up in a band from your bank- to your coin dealer. Buy one 1 oz. American Eagle gold coin, and the rest in silver coins and bars. You want to buy normal eagles, whatever the most recent minting of coins are; don't buy collector coins if they offer them to you, as you're buying metals to be used as money.

Here's a really important point: As long as you're buying under $10,000 worth of metals at a time, they don't need to see your ID; you can buy those metals with full privacy. The moment you buy $10,000+ of metals, they have to report the purchase to the IRS. I've gone to my local precious metals dealer with $9000 cash before, and had a young worker that was new ask me for my ID.

I told him calmly, *"You don't need my ID. If I was buying over $10,000 worth of metals, you would need my ID to report the purchase to the IRS. As I* *am buying $9000 worth of metals, please simply give me a receipt and write '$9000 cash' as payment on the receipt, leaving the customer name section blank. For future reference, you don't need anyone's ID for sales under $10,000."*

If the worker is still confused, simply tell them *"I want to maintain my privacy for this purchase."* **If they won't write up your receipt this way, kindly ask to speak with their manager**.

Once you buy your metals, put them in a bag when you leave the store. You can bring a backpack with you or a canvas shopping bag, and put your metals in there; that way, it isn't obvious to someone that you have metals in the bag. Once you go home, put your metals in your safe with your cash. Those are your best practices for buying and storing your precious metals.

I'm going to give you another key strategy which is this: how do you MOST wisely diversify your investments, knowing that misfortune can happen on the earth? *First of all, know that money in mutual funds is being used by BlackRock, Vanguard, and State Street to steal your wealth.*

Those funds are basically carrying out the WEF Agenda 2030 of *"you'll own nothing and be happy"* by the year 2030. They're buying up real estate like crazy. They are using loaning money to businesses through ESG funds to try to control those companies. **So, I humbly suggest you do NOT invest your money into companies that are literally planning to impoverish you.**

On one hand, they're paying you 8% to 10% on your money. On the other hand, their plan is to steal ALL of your wealth. So don't harm yourself with your investments. Knowing that Blackrock, Vanguard, & State Street control over $10 Trillion and are the majority shareholders in 88% of all publicly traded companies in the world, how do you NOT support them? It's a challenge, because they have their tentacles in almost the whole global financial system.

One way is to do research and find smaller publicly traded companies that they haven't invested in. **Another way to make sure the WEF is not using your wealth against you is the following....**

Protection Strategy #4:

Invest in private companies.

These days, when you're experiencing inflation over 10% stealing your purchasing power, it's vital you find safe ways to earn a lot more than 8% or 10%, safely and conservatively, compared to the stock market's wild swings. Investing in commercial real estate and private businesses that pay cash flow are two great strategies I recommend you implement ASAP.

You can invest in private companies directly with money that is currently in stocks, bonds, or cash; you can also invest with funds from IRAs and old 401Ks, through self-directed IRA administrators like TrustETC.com.

Here are a couple key pointers for self-directing your retirement funds (your IRA or Roth IRA in the USA, and your Super fund in the UK/Australia): The first step is to move your funds from a traditional administrator (that only lets you invest in mutual funds, stocks, and bonds) to a self-directed retirement account administrator. If you have a 401k from an old job that you're not working at, you can convert that to an IRA, and you can self-direct those investment funds as well.

Once your funds are moved over, next you tell (or "*direct*") your new retirement account administrator where to invest your funds. **You can invest your retirement funds in real estate, gold and silver, and stocks of private companies.**

One asset class I would recommend passively investing in is commercial real estate- apartments, office buildings, self-storage units, and strip malls. You can invest in REITs (Real Estate Investment Trusts), groups of investors that buy a property together (called syndicates), and you can also invest directly with individual commercial real estate investors.

Most of these investments will pay you cash flow, and a lot of real estate deals can pay you 8% to 12% or more per year in annual cash flow. Depending on how the deal is structured, in addition to the cashflow you earn, you can often earn a percentage of the increased value of the property when it sells, and get good tax breaks annually from commercial real estate as well.

To give you an idea, a guy I met at a conference is paying some of his investors 12% to 18% per year in profits, because he's buying houses and converting them into assisted living facilities for elderly people, and they are earning amazing cash flow on those properties.

You can also invest in private businesses that produce cash flow, even with your IRA and Superfund self-directed accounts. You can invest in established businesses, or even in startup businesses that have the potential to pay you cash flow or a large ROI quickly.

Before going deeper into the keys to success investing in private companies, I want to reiterate the overall goal of modeling King Solomon's trillionaire wisdom strategy of, "Divide your money into 7 or 8 (assets),

for you do not know what misfortune will happen on the Earth:"

For your diversified investment portfolio of private companies, real estate, and metals, I recommend the following: for every $1M you invest, put $300K to $400K into real estate, $300K to $400K into private businesses, and $200K to $300K into metals.

(To clarify regarding metals, you don't take possession of the metals you buy in your IRA or Super account; I'm recommending you have 20% of your IRA investment funds in metals in ADDITION to the metals you keep in your safe)

When it comes to investing in businesses, I wanted to give you one MAJOR KEY POINTER for buying stock in a private company with your IRA or your Super funds: <u>you need to invest in OTHER people's companies</u>. You can't set up an LLC and buy a property with that LLC, using your own IRA money.

That's called self-dealing, and it will cause you to have to pay a big penalty, PLUS upfront taxes. Don't play with fire; stay on the good side of the law when self-directing your retirement funds and invest in other people's deals/companies.

When you're investing in private companies, look for teams of people with relevant experience, ideally that can start paying you cash flow fairly quickly. WAY more important than the company's business model is the team's ability to execute and be flexible. Also, look for a track record of overcoming obstacles, either in the leadership team OR in the company's advisory board, like Steve Jobs (& Wozniacki) had when starting Apple.

Also, look for companies that can start paying you revenue within a year, where your stock is sellable within 1-2 years. Some pre-IPO startups lock up funds for as much as 3-5 years. Avoid that scenario and keep your money liquid, where if the company isn't doing well within 1-2 years, you can sell the stock and put your money into something else.

In summary, when buying private stock: look for a team with relevant experience (or experienced advisors), avoid your money being locked up for any longer than 1-2 years, and look for deals that can start paying you cashflow within 1 year.

Protection Strategy #5:
(BONUS) Hold digital dollars and digital gold & silver

Earlier in this chapter, I spoke about the strategies of addressing banking risk by holding physical cash and physical gold and silver. **What if you want to convert $10M+ to metals and cash, OR you want to spend some of your metals or cash internationally?** That can be quite challenging.

You can only carry $10K cash with you internationally, and you have to declare any amount of cash over $10K on customs forms when traveling internationally; that exposes you to the risk of confiscation by an under-informed officer of the law & thieves, and you lose the privacy of cash.

You face the same risks when carrying over $10K of physical gold & silver coins internationally. It can be a pain to spend $100K+ of cash and metals domestically as well. If you want to invest in a business or buy an asset worth $100K+ in another state, you risk confiscation and theft of them as well.

To address these risks, I encourage you to **buy some digital gold and digital cash**, to go along with your physical cash and physical metals. Spend your physical cash and metals locally when you want privacy for your transactions, and I encourage you to spend cash at as many local vendors as possible for those reasons as well.

When you want to buy something far away with privacy, you can safely pay for them with digital cash and digital gold and silver.

The most widely used digital cash is USDT – called Tether; it's tied to the price of the US dollar, and floats in price between $1.02 and $0.98 per 1 Tether. Tether is not only the most widely used stablecoin in the USA; it's also used by most people globally that want to hold digital US dollars. In Africa, for example, most technology workers prefer to be paid in Tether.

There are a couple vendors you can buy digital gold and silver through: the ones I have experience with are Vaultoro.com and Paxos, and they are a couple of the biggest sellers of digital gold and digital silver (digital tokens backed by gold and silver bars and coins). Whenever you buy gold or silver through them, the transaction is on the blockchain, and they buy the physical metal to back your digital coins.

The main challenge with digital dollars and digital precious metals, is that it is not 100% clear that they have a 1:1 backing for all of the tokens they've issued. For example, at this moment you don't know if there is $1M in the bank for every $1M of Tether sold to the public.

In essence you have to trust them, much like you have to trust companies that sell gold ETFs or central banks that tell us they have X amount of gold bullion backing up the currency they're issuing, as most central banks have not had their gold reserves independently audited since the 1950's.

The other challenge with digital tokens backed by physical gold and silver is that the global demand for the metals is growing rapidly, and is much greater than the amount of gold and silver that's available to buy. Silver is used in most electronics today, and more of it is being used per year than is being mined from the Earth. Gold is used in jewelry and industry, AND central banks are buying all the gold they can get their hands on, so as an individual investor you're competing with them to buy physical gold.

Put simply, there is only enough gold above ground for each person in the world to own 1 ounce of it, and the amount of gold available for you to buy now is going down as central banks buy more and more of it. How can this challenge be solved?

One solution that will greatly enhance trust in, and adoption of, digital dollars and digital metals is more transparency confirming the amount of actual assets that are backing them. Another solution is to expand on the amount of gold and silver that can be tokenized, by tokenizing it while it's still in the ground.

Companies that build the technology stack to accurately, affordably, and efficiently measure the amount of gold that is in the ground, and tokenize that gold in a way that's 100% compliant with existing securities regulations worldwide, will be able to GREATLY expand the amount of gold available for people to buy globally, and thus protect their wealth.

That is what our company **www.GoldPlusCoin.com** *is doing currently; we have $6B of in-ground gold under contract to buy now, and another $20B+ of gold we can buy. Our goal is to tokenize $100B+ of in- ground gold in the next 3-5 years, to help people preserve their purchasing power even if their local currency is devalued, and to help protect the wealth they've worked so hard to acquire.*

Last but not least, I want to share a rare opportunity with you. We've raised funds for GoldPlusCoin.com already, and we're raising another $10M to $100M to bring our product to market. Within 6 months of us getting over the $10M funding level, our Gold Plus Coin ("*GPC*") tokens should be available to retail buyers worldwide, and you can buy some.

To be among the FIRST people in the world that have an opportunity to hold GPC as part of your physical gold and digital gold portfolio, join our newsletter mailing list by entering your information at www.GoldPlusCoin.com.

I encourage you to go forth and prosper as your soul prospers, friend! **Take massive action; look over your notes from this chapter, consider the best next steps for YOU to take addressing bank risk and investment risk.**

Put some funds into cash and metals, and start looking for some private companies and real estate to invest in, that can pay you cash flow ASAP. Doing these things, you'll be better protected than 99% of your peers from the WEF Agenda 2030 and other financial uncertainties, and you can be at peace and sleep better accordingly.

No matter what strategies you employ, don't be like the fool that King Solomon describes, who sees danger ahead and yet keeps going in the same direction. Take new precautionary actions like other wise people are doing, and you and your family will benefit accordingly.

I wish you much success, and I'm excited to hear your results as you take action with these strategies.

CHAPTER 5

"Get Back IN There and Sell, Sell, SELL!!!"

Do you recognize the above statement? I'll give you a hint: frozen orange juice. Still scratching your head? It's from the movie *"Trading Places"* starring Eddie Murphy and Dan Akroyd. It's one of my favorite movies of all time because it's very funny and one of very few movies about commodities trading.

In the scene where the quote comes from, two *"Lolo"* owners of a commodities trading firm- the Duke brothers- attempt to corner the orange juice market by buying a copy of its crops report before it comes out to the public.

Their plan gets sabotaged, so they think the cost of orange juice will go up and buy tens of millions of dollars of contracts betting "*long*" for higher prices. When the actual report comes out, the price drops very quickly, there's a selling frenzy and the Duke brothers' trader can't sell their contracts fast enough to contain their losses. At the end of the trading day they owe the commodities exchange $850 Million and are instantly bankrupted.

The movie teaches many important lessons. First, it shows the pitfalls of greed; the Duke brothers wipe out all the wealth they've acquired in their lifetimes with one very bad decision. Second, it demonstrates the importance of timing in your investments. You can be right about where a market is heading and still go broke if you buy into the market the wrong way, too early, or too late.

There are many factors that affect who you should sell your precious metals to and how you sell them to make sure you maximize your profits. As such, I'll review the when, who, and how to for each main category of sellers you may belong to one by one.

Seller Group #1: Individuals with Bullion

If you're an individual owning your gold and silver in bullion coins like American Eagles and bullion bars, then the main factors involved for you are timing and who to sell to.

The best time for you to sell your bullion is when it will buy the most assets possible at cheap prices (remember your target is to increase the value of your wealth). This will be at the end of a Seller Stage 4 cycle or the start of a Buyer Stage 1 cycle. Once you own bullion, I strongly recommend you subscribe to WealthCycles.com to time your sales.

As far as who to sell your bullion to, your 2 best options in the Philippines are selling it back to your coin broker or directly to the BSP's Metals Division.

GoldSilver.com will buy bullion back from you at the market price and will buy all the coins and bars you want to sell them. Make sure you get input from a GoldSilver.com agent on how to properly label, pack, and insure your package of bullion you send them. You will receive your wired payment from them within 3 business days of them receiving your package, so with priority shipping you can get paid in full within 7 to 10 days.

Your second option is to sell your bullion to the BSP. They will also pay you market price for your bullion, and they have 5 buying stations in the Philippines located in Quezon City, Baguio, Davao,

Zamboanga, and Naga City. (BSP Locations: bsp.gov.ph/contact/regional.asp)

According to Roque Rubiano in the BSP Quezon City Metals Division, they'll charge you 7% taxes upfront (2% excise tax and 5% holding tax for the BIR), and they'll pay you 80% within 1 day of receiving your metal via direct transfer to your bank account and the remaining 20% due to you within 30 days.

A third factor to consider when selling your bullion is time vs. cost/convenience. If the cost to ship and insure a package to a coin broker like GoldSilver is less than the 7% tax the BSP will charge you upfront, you may want to sell to a coin broker. On the other hand, if you have the opportunity to buy a great cash-flowing asset like an apartment building for a bargain price and need the cash in 5 days, it may make more sense for you to sell your bullion to the BSP if you're near a BSP metals buying station. (BSP Buying Guidelines: bsp.gov.ph/bspnotes/bspgold.asp)

Seller Group #2: Miners/Traders

As I stated earlier in the book, the Philippines is the 6th-most mineral rich country in the world and its mining sector is only operating at 17% of its capacity, so this equates to HUGE opportunities for profit with the right team and strategies in place.

In speaking with multiple miners and traders in the Philippines, I and my team have discovered that the #1 way to expand your profits as a miner or gold trader is to work with a buyer that will ADD VALUE to your operation, not just pay you a slightly higher price.

For example, if you're a small-scale miner, by law you have to sell your supply to the BSP. One way a buyer can add value to you is to help you upgrade your equipment so that you can mine more gold/hour. Upgraded tools may increase your income by 10% up to 20%.

If you operate a grinder or refine gold into dust form, a buyer can add value to you by helping you upgrade your equipment as well- by either extracting gold out of the rocks miners bring you faster or in larger quantities. For example, some equipment using laser or sonic technology can extract up to 30% to 50% more gold from rocks because it can separate gold from the rock in smaller sizes.

If you deliver gold disks for the BSP to financiers, a buyer can add value to you by helping you streamline your pickup and delivery routes and processes modeling the best practices of LBC, DHL, or UPS. This can enable you to do 10-20% more deliveries/month.

Lastly, if you're a financier the right strategic buyer can help you turn your money over the fastest for maximum profit. My company, for example, helps some clients boost their profits by 5% or so almost overnight using one of our little-known techniques.

I see great potential in the Philippine gold mining industry at the small & medium scales to model Blockbuster Video's or Waste Management's buyout strategy or Wal-Mart's distribution process streamlining strategy that can lead to HUGE profit increases for you in PI mining- if you're ambitious, have vision, and are willing to do the work.

Seller Group #3: Pawnshops and Jewelers

Besides miners, pawnshops and jewelers are the largest sellers of gold to the BSP. That makes sense as so much jewelry is sold and pawned/not redeemed to them daily. Whether you follow the Cebuana model of retailing most of the jewelry you get or you follow the Villarica model of quickly selling your gold jewelry to the BSP or another buyer, you should always consider selling part of your supply quickly so you can turn your money over quickly. Making PHP300,000 4 times/yr is more profitable than making PHP500,000 2 times/yr using the same business funds.

Some in the pawnshop industry and miners have expressed concern to me that they may be losing part of their metal in the BSP's refining process itself. I don't know whether these concerns are valid or not.

A simple way to find out would be to split a lot of 10Kg or 20Kg of 14K, 18K, or 22K jewelry and sell half to the BSP and half to a buyer with a 1st-class global refinery account. If one gives you more yield than the other, then you have your answer.

Seller Group #4: Family Heirloom Holders

There are many amazing stories of treasure finds, treasure hunts, and buried bunkers filled with booty all over the Philippines. From the Spanish Era to Yamashita's gold, there are some amazing tales indeed! I remember on a trip to Cagayan de Oro being fascinated as my Cagayan River rapids guide told me of some treasure finds in a cave above the river.

It's easy to dismiss those stories as purely fictional, or to believe them 100%. After me and my team seeing and verifying the purity of multiple bars from 3 holders at 90%+ pure, it's clear they came from somewhere!

No matter where it came from, there are some Filipinos holding real gold bars, and the stories only make the process of owning, selling, and buying them more fun.

I have heard some holders of this type of gold consider it to be holy. If you think this way, I caution you to remember how God almost destroyed the Israelites for worshipping a golden calf idol instead of Him. Only God is holy and deserves worship, the Bible tells us.

No matter where it came from, if it's in your hands then God wants you to be a good steward of the resources He's entrusted to you. If you've been watching over multiple gold bars for 5, 10, or 20+ years, is it wise to keep doing so? As I've clearly showed you in the previous chapters, it does you little good in heirloom form; I humbly suggest you convert some of it to cash and bullion now before hyperinflation hits.

If you're reading this, you're more likely to know someone who claims to have heirloom gold than hold it yourself. As such, use the following checklist to help you determine both which sellers and buyers are worth your time to work with. If a buyer or seller is unwilling to obey the law and use safe procedures, then don't work with them no matter how much money or gold they have.

God rewards integrity and wisdom, and no amount of money is worth trading your soul for!

As gold is strictly regulated, it's very important you follow all PI and international laws regarding its purchase and sale.

Here are the 4 biggest challenges heirloom gold holders face and how to address them:

1. Stay safe- When transporting: Don't tell anyone when/where you're going, and bring proper paperwork with you showing you're authorized to carry the gold. I've heard of multiple people not arriving at their destination or being detained because they didn't have proper paperwork and were accused of stealing gold and arrested. When meeting: Always meet/discuss a sale to potential buyers in public. Only after you've built trust should you meet in private to test bars/do a contract.

2. Avoid going to jail. If you're transporting gold either domestically or internationally, you need paperwork showing you're the rightful owner of it or authorizing you to transport it. Taking your gold to get tested or sell some of it without a Proof of Origin, Certificate of Ownership, or Authorization to Carry paperwork is very foolish and potentially VERY dangerous.

   If the authorities question you as to where

your gold came from and you don't have proof you own it or are acting on the owner's behalf, you'll be put in jail at minimum and might even end up being interrogated or tortured for information. I always think the best of people and love all pinoys; accurate thinking dictates that if 600+ PI journalists could go missing or be killed in the 2000s, then you could definitely disappear over a few gold bars worth $1,000,000.

Stay safe; don't carry large amounts of gold at all until you have the proper paperwork.

3. Avoid being cheated- both when assaying and when being paid. Assaying- get more than one assay to verify your gold's purity for the first time (a great strategy is to go to multiple pawn shops in 1 day), and when signing a contract with a buyer have the metal wrapped in the assay report. I've heard many first-hand stories from holders who have been cheated or stolen from by pawn shops or small refinery buyers; look for an assayer that is BSP-licensed that will give you a written assay report with their signature on it.

Being paid- beware buyers who come offering big deposits in cash. They'll entice you to sell them 5 or 10 bars with a sizable deposit, but then disappear. This happened to one seller I met a few years back; beware this trickery!

Another trick is to show you proof of funds but not pay you once they get your gold OR to give you an all cash payment leading you to get intercepted by authorities with the cash.

This happened to a holder I met with last year; he went with a buyer to their refinery in their country, and when attempting to leave the country with his cash he was intercepted. Perhaps the buyer tipped the authorities off to get his cash back after a "*commission.*" Needless to say, the holder was lucky he didn't go to jail for customs violations.

Bottom line: if a buyer pays you all cash, they're breaking both PI and international law and you should RUN from them.

Legit buyers have nothing to hide; they'll let you come with them to their refinery and go with them to their bank when they pay you your deposit and the balance due. Only deal with legit buyers who are open, honest, and will comply with all international and PI laws so they can do multiple transactions with you. This is how you keep from being cheated.

4. Avoid your money being frozen. I have spoken to several gold sellers who asked to be paid in cash, and it's almost always been for 2 main reasons. Either they want privacy, they don't have a bank account so they don't trust banks (it's normal to fear the unknown), or both.

Let's look at the international laws concerning the sale of gold so the gold holders you know can obey the laws, still maintain their privacy, and hold some of their money in cash. Gold is one of the most regulated commodities in the world. In order to bring gold to a refinery (which all legitimate, smart buyers will do), you need to have a license or some form of ID and a bank account. The reason why is that the refinery must pay you via wire transfer or direct deposit so that the sale can be tracked and the gold legitimized. This is vital to reduce- and prevent when possible- money laundering and other criminal activities.

So, we've established that you need an ID and a bank account to sell to a refinery.

Also, you need an ID to validate your signature

when you sign your Sales Agreement with your buyer. You want to know who you're selling to, right? Well, your buyer wants to know who they're buying from too.

Let me walk you through the different parts of a legitimate sale of your gold in reverse so you see why the contract, bank account, ID, and Proof of Origin are all needed.

Your buyer takes your gold to their refinery to be paid for it. The refinery asks where the gold came from, so your buyer shows them your signed contract, ID, and Proof of Origin.

The refinery pays your buyer and you get paid via bank wire as well. Your bank asks where the money came from, so you show them your contract and assay report from the refinery. Also when your buyer's bank asks him where he's wiring the funds, he shows them your signed contract and ID.

To comply with the Philippines Anti-Money Laundering Act (AMLA), your buyer pays you a deposit of PHP350,000 to obey the AMLA RA9160 rule (a copy of it is in the Resources section) that you can't receive a deposit any bigger than PHP500,000 for the sale of money or precious metals as gold is both. You show the bank your contract as soon as you receive your deposit so they know you're expecting a larger amount of funds coming in.

When your buyer pays their taxes, they're able to pay income taxes only on the difference between the price they bought from you and sold at by providing your contract as proof of their net profits. This one is a BIG deal that many sellers and buyers don't think about.

Do the math: if your buyer buys from you at 60% LBMA and sells it to their refinery for 80% LBMA, they make a 20% spread. With the contract, they pay 20% taxes on their 20% profit or 4% tax total. If you DIDN'T have a contract, then the government would think they made the full 80% as profit and tax them at 20% of 80% or 16% total tax. Without a contract, your buyer would only make a net 4% profit after taxes.

So, to summarize this section you can see why having a contract that complies with all PI and international laws governing AMLA and the sale of gold protects both you and your buyer.

If you're a family heirloom gold holder and you absolutely don't want your name on a Sales Agreement, you can still sell your gold as long as there's someone in your group you trust to sign the contract and receive payments on your behalf.

Remember from the previous chapters that once you get paid via bank wire, it won't be wise to withdraw all your funds out of the bank as cash in Pesos due to inflation. You'll want to buy some gold and silver bullion bars and coins that are internationally recognized, and since you'll already have a bank account you'll be able to buy your bullion coins right away as well as withdraw some cash.

*A final note on keeping your money from getting frozen by the banks: if NO ONE in your holder's group has an Identification Card, you can get one in 2 days. Have whoever you trust that will sign the contract for you go to their Barangay captain to get a barangay ID, and have them take their barangay ID to the nearest post office to get a Postal ID. They can complete the whole process in 1 day, and then they can sign the contract to sell gold for you using their ID.

Is Finding All These Things in A Buyer Too Good To Be True?

Great question. And it's fair one too. In speaking with many Filipino gold owners, my experience is that there aren't many buyers out there playing by all the rules. Some of them are knowingly breaking PI and international laws governing the purchase of gold, and they're willing to take that risk all for the sake of greed.

Just so you know, you CAN find buyers who will deal fairly with you and obey the law. If you're a miner or family heirloom gold holder, I encourage you not to give up hope finding an honest buyer to work with no matter how many dishonest or shortsighted people you run across in your business dealings.

****

To sum up this chapter, even though your profit is made when you buy an asset, it is vital that you sell your gold and silver the right way at the best time following the right procedures so you can REALIZE massive profits with your gold and silver holdings.

CHAPTER 6

Conclusion: So What is the Golden Opportunity Before You Now?
That depends on you.

My dear friend, I trust this book has helped open your eyes to the financial mess the world is in; I also trust it has empowered you to face the challenges before you today head-on with power, might, and strength by God's grace.

Most of our world leaders have let us down, but you have the knowledge and strategies in your hands to NOW create wealth no matter what the government does! Choose today to be joyful as you apply the wisdom of King Solomon in your finances with this book.

I know I've laid out some radical concepts in this book that defy conventional wisdom; heck, many or most of the ideas I've shared with you may fly in the face of everything you've been taught to this point.

I hope I've challenged you to think independently with this book; thinking like the *"sheeple"* (the vast majority of people who are easily led and simply follow the crowd) will leave you broke and scrambling for financial solutions when it will probably be too late to help you. It's not enough to think new things; you must now become new.

Use the concepts in this book to improve your finances. Start to change the way you think about money and search for mentors and MasterMind partners to hold you accountable as you seek a better life for yourself. Invest time and money to stay informed about what's happening in the financial world so you will be a more educated investor- an investment in yourself is always worth every penny.

Invest in WealthCycles.com- split the cost with a few friends if you have to!- and make sure to buy as many silver and coins as you can in the next couple/few years while we're still in this Seller Phase 3 wealth cycle. Also, get some digital gold and digital dollars, and buy shares in some cashflowing private businesses as outlined in chapter 4. The more you diversify your holdings to reduce your risk, the better!

Take action with what you've learned here despite your fear. Fear of failure, fear of success, fear of the unknown- it's all the same and you need to work through it. Every successful person has taken action despite their fears; you're a successful person, right? I thought so. Ask God to strengthen you to take action in the midst of fear, and He will.

It's normal to be afraid to try something different. No one wants to be the *"odd man out,"* and I'll tell you now you're going to be mocked by some of your friends when you implement this book's strategies. You know what I say? Take responsibility for your finances, forgive their ignorance, and reap the rewards! Gift them a copy of this book too.

I trust I've given you enough strategies and pointed you to enough additional resources in this book to feel empowered to face each new day's challenges with hope.

If after everything I've shared with you here, you still find yourself struggling with doubt or fear, I encourage you to put your hope in the One who never fails or will let you down- the Lord Jesus Christ. I was one day away from suicide when I stopped trying to overcome my kleptomania in my own strength and accepted Christ. After 4 years of attempting to overcome my addiction on my own and failing, Jesus healed me instantly overnight! I want you to experience that same power and hope for the future in your life too.

"For by grace have you been saved through faith, and this not from yourselves, it is the gift of God- not by works, so that no one can boast." –Ephesians 2:8,9 Meditate on those verses so you can stop hoping you're good enough to be accepted by God the Father and start knowing you are through Christ alone.

Only 2%-4% of the people reading this book will actually take action to improve their lives financially and spiritually. Will you be one of them? Only you can decide. Choose wisely.

When you do take action, you'll be able to boldly say, *"I have found the ultimate treasure in the Treasure Islands!!"*

May God richly reward your diligence with his grace and favor, my friend.

Wala na, kaibigan!!

(OFWs: *"That's it, friend!!"*)

THAT'S ALMOST IT...

Following is a Resource Section containing several of the references I made throughout this book and financial tools for your benefit. Enjoy and put them to use!

RESOURCES

To Optimize The Way You Think:

"*Think and Grow Rich*" by Dr. Napoleon Hill

"*The Science of Getting Rich*" by Wallace Wattles (Get your FREE copies of these classics online by DuckDuckGo searching their titles)

(www.Psycho-Cybernetics.com)

"*Rich Dad Poor Dad*" by Robert Kiyosaki

"*The CASHFLOW Quadrant™*" by Robert Kiyosaki

"*Rich Dad's Classics*" by Robert Kiyosaki

   (get either at **http://www.RichDad.com**)

To Live a Balanced Life in Every Way:

"*Passion, Profit, and Power*" by Marshall Sylver

   (**www.Sylver.com**)

Entrepinoy Foundation- this group provides mentoring and strategic support to pinoy entrepreneurs growing or starting PI businesses (www.Entrepinoy.org)

To Get Great Consulting and Support For Starting a Business:

"GoNegosyo"— founded by Joey Concepcion, this group encourages Filipinos to go into business and connects them with MANY resources to help them make their businesses succeed like microfinance, business planning tools, marketing tools, etc. (**GoNegosyo.net**)

S.C.O.R.E. aka Service Corps Of Retired Executives (http://Score.org) — this organization has a number of retired executives and business owners who can give you wise counsel on starting, structuring, financing, and running your own business

My Favorite Charities That Focus on Building God's Kingdom (by giving to charity, you set in motion the law of reciprocity; what you give out will always come back to you multiplied):

Center for Community Transformation (www. CCT.org.Ph/new) — they give small business loans to poor people in the Philippines to help them start their own small businesses. These are people that banks won't give loans to because they *"don't qualify"* yet CCT has a 98% repayment of loans! CCT also provides loans for affordable housing as well as scholarships for poor students. A charity that is truly empowering people- learn more at their website!

Voice of the Martyrs (www.Persecution.com) — they provide support to the persecuted Church mainly in the 10/40 window where there are few Christians. They sneak Bibles to people in countries where they're illegal, support pastors in countries hostile to Christianity, and provide vital prayer support. Amen!

Focus on the Family (www.Family.org) — Started by Dr. James Dobson, Focus does radio broadcasts in over 100 countries around the world to strengthen families. A vital charity that brings families closer together when many forces are weakening families.

Advancing Native Missions (www.ADNAMIS.org) — support native missionaries that go to remote and dangerous places to share Christ's love with them.

EndPoverty.org — give microloans to people help start businesses in 20+ countries. Amazing!

*The next few pages are copies of Philippines government documents showing that pinoys are allowed to transport their family heirloom gold with government protection, pinoys are legally allowed to export gold out of the country, and documentation verifying my company CDO Gold's account with NTR Metals refinery and when payment will be received for any metal we bring them.

Put fear of the unknown behind you and now focus on opportunities in front of you!

114 | RESOURCES

Verification You Can Export Gold from the PI

Circular Letters

Date Issued: 06.25.1999

CIRCULAR LETTER
Series of 1999

TO : All Authorized Agent Banks and All Concerned

S U B J E C T : Exportation of Gold and Nickel Babbitt

Please be advised that under CB Circular No. 1389 dated 13 April 1999, as amended, the following commodities may be exported without need for prior clearance from BSP:

1. Gold in any form including gold bars and dore metal, except panned gold or gold from small-scale mining which is required to be sold to BSP ; and

2. Nickel Babbitt.

Please inform your exporter-clients of this Circular-Letter and that there is no further need to get specific letter confirmation of this from the BSP.

FOR THE MONETARY BOARD:

EDGARDO P. ZIALCITA
Deputy Governor

This Circular Letter dated June 25, 1999, states in Item #1 that *"Please be advised that the following commodities may be exported without need for prior clearance from BSP: Gold in any form including gold bars and dore metal, except panned gold or gold from small-scale mining which is required to be sold to BSP."*

(from bsp.gov.ph/regulations/regulations.asp?type=2&id=529)

PI Government Republic Act 9160

REPUBLIC ACT NO. 9160

(as amended by Republic Act No. 9194)

AN ACT DEFINING THE CRIME OF MONEY LAUNDERING, PROVIDING PENALTIES THEREFOR AND FOR OTHER PURPOSES

Be it enacted by the Senate and House of Representatives of the Philippines in Congress assembled:

SECTION 1. *Short Title.* – This Act shall be known as the "Anti-Money Laundering Act of 2001."

SEC. 2. *Declaration of Policy.* – It is hereby declared the policy of the State to protect and preserve the integrity and confidentiality of bank accounts and to ensure that the Philippines shall not be used as a money laundering site for the proceeds of any unlawful activity. Consistent with its foreign policy, the State shall extend cooperation in transnational investigations and prosecutions of persons involved in money laundering activities wherever committed.

SEC. 3. *Definitions.* – For purposes of this Act, the following terms are hereby defined as follows:

(a) "Covered institution" refers to:

(1) banks, non-banks, quasi-banks, trust entities, and all other institutions and their subsidiaries and affiliates supervised or regulated by the Bangko Sentral ng Pilipinas (BSP);

(2) insurance companies and all other institutions supervised or regulated by the Insurance Commission; and

(3) (i) securities dealers, brokers, salesmen, investment houses and other similar entities managing securities or rendering services as investment agent, advisor, or consultant, (ii) mutual funds, close-end investment companies, common trust funds, pre-need companies and other similar entities, (iii) foreign exchange corporations, money changers, money payment, remittance, and transfer companies and other similar entities, and (iv) other entities administering or otherwise dealing in currency, commodities or financial derivatives based thereon, valuable objects, cash substitutes and other similar monetary instruments or property supervised or regulated by Securities and Exchange Commission.

(b) 'Covered transaction' is a transaction in cash or other equivalent monetary instrument involving a total amount in excess of Five hundred thousand pesos (P500,000.00) within one (1) banking day.

(b-1) 'Suspicious transaction' are transactions with covered institutions, regardless of the amounts involved, where any of the following circumstances exist:

This states in Section 3iv: "*Covered institution*" refers to: entities dealing in currency, commodities... or cash substitutes.

In Section 3b it states: "*Covered transaction*" is a transaction... in excess of P500,000.00

Translation: if you're selling gold, you're a covered institution governed by AMLA and any transaction over P500,000 they'll investigate and can freeze your money over if you don't have the proper documentation. We have the needed documents.

PI Government Republic Act 9160 page 2

1. there is no underlying legal or trade obligation, purpose

2. the client is not properly identified;

3. the amount involved is not commensurate with the bus the client;

4. taking into account all known circumstances, it may b- transaction is structured in order to avoid being the subjec under the Act;

5. any circumstance relating to the transaction which is c profile of the client and/or the client's past transactions with th

6. the transaction is in any way related to an unlawful acti that is about to be, is being or has been committed; or

7. any transaction that is similar or analogous to any of the

(c) "Monetary instrument" refers to:

(1) coins or currency of legal tender of the Philippines, or of an

(2) drafts, checks and notes;

(3) securities or negotiable instruments, bonds, commercial pa certificates, custodial receipts or deposit substitute instruments, tra and confirmations of sale or investments and money market instrun

(4) other similar instruments where title thereto passes assignment or delivery.

Section 3b1 (2) states: *"Suspicious transactions"* are transactions where any of the following circumstances exist: the client is not properly identified.

This is why when selling your heirloom gold you need a copy of both your ID and your buyer's ID as well as a valid contract complying with both PI and international law. We have a way to help you obey the law AND still maintain your privacy selling your gold. To my knowledge, our group is the only buyer in the Philippines giving gold holders this combination of vital solutions.

PI Government Republic Act 9160 page 5

> The provisions of existing laws to the contrary notwithstanding, anonymous accounts, accounts under fictitious names, and all other similar accounts shall be absolutely prohibited. Peso and foreign currency non-checking numbered accounts shall be allowed. The BSP may conduct annual testing solely limited to the determination of the existence and true identity of the owners of such accounts.
>
> (b) Record Keeping. – All records of all transactions of covered institutions shall be maintained and safely stored for five (5) years from the dates of transactions. With respect to closed accounts, the records on customer identification, account files and business correspondence, shall be preserved and safely stored for at least five (5) years from the dates when they were closed.
>
> (c) Reporting of Covered and Suspicious Transactions.[8] – Covered institutions shall report to the AMLC all covered transactions and suspicious transactions within five (5) working days from occurrence thereof, unless the Supervising Authority prescribes a longer period not exceeding ten (10) working days.
>
> Should a transaction be determined to be both a covered transaction and a suspicious transaction, the covered institution shall be required to report the same as a suspicious transaction.
>
> When reporting covered or suspicious transactions to the AMLC, covered institutions and their officers and employees [representatives, agents, advisors, consultants or associates] shall not be deemed to have violated Republic Act No. 1405, as amended, Republic Act No. 6426, as amended, Republic Act No. 8791 and other similar laws, but are prohibited from communicating, directly or indirectly, in any manner or by any means, to any person, the fact that a covered or suspicious transaction report was made, the contents thereof, or any other information in relation thereto. In case of violation thereof, the concerned officer and employee [, representative, agent, advisor, consultant or associate] of the covered institution shall be criminally liable. However, no administrative, criminal or civil proceedings, shall lie against any person for having made a

Section 9c states: *Covered institutions (banks) shall report to the AMLC all covered transactions and suspicious transactions within five (5) working days from occurance thereof*

Translation: Your bank only has to report a transaction in your account if it looks suspicious. To avoid this, when you receive your wire from the buyer of your gold you simply provide your bank manager with a copy of your Sales Agreement so they know where your deposit funds came from. The AMLA division of your bank will automatically review any transaction over P500,000, so you need a banker that knows these guidelines –like ours- so your account won't be frozen from a large sale. After that, you can withdraw the funds in cash (and convert at least half of it into bullion coins if you're smart).

CDO GOLD LLC Account Verification Letter from NTR Metals

September 2, 2011

NTR Metals, LLC
10720 Composite Drive
Dallas, TX 75220

To Whom It May Concern:

Please be advised that the following client has an account with NTR Metals, LLC[#]:

CDO Gold, LLC
David Newby
3319 Greenfield Rd. #369
Dearborn, MI 48120

NTR will provide refining services for precious metal it purchases from CDO Gold, LLC and payment will be made within 24 – 48 hours (2 business days) of the metal's arrival, assay, refinement, and final assay.

Sincerely,

NTR Metals, LLC

Morgan Lewis
In-House Counsel

The letter states: *"NTR will provide refining services for precious metal it purchases from GDO Gold LLC, and payment will be made within 24-48 hours (2 business days) of the metal's arrival, assay, refinement, and final assay. Sincerely, NTR Metals, Morgan Lewis, In-House Counsel"* – this is PROOF that you'll be wired your funds in 2-3 business days as soon as NTR Metals releases our funds.

If you sell us gold domestically in the Philippines, we'll pay you in full within 24 hours of receiving your items and taking them to one of our refineries.

NTR Refining Statement for Gold Sample CDO GOLD Brought to Their San Francisco office

 NTR Metals

The gold that was brought in tested at 99.6% pure gold. Also, the NOTES section says this:

9/19/11: International transactions approved for Philippines only... no other countries have been approved.

We brought this sample over from one of the 3 real gold bars we've tested from PI heirloom gold owners.

NOTES:

NOTES:

www.ingramcontent.com/pod-product-compliance
Lightning Source LLC
Chambersburg PA
CBHW020432220526
45464CB00002B/675